"The hope must be that the School will still be here in 2012 so that the same traditions and talent can be acclaimed by whoever takes up his pen – or plugs in his word processor – to celebrate its 100th Anniversary" Keith Nodding, Head Master, writing at the time of the 75th Anniversary in 1987.

The History of Altrincham Grammar School for Boys from 1912-2012

Celebrating a Centenary

Author: G. Murray. **Designer**: D. Nicholl-Timmins. **Editor**: T. J. Gartside.

Thanks go to all who have helped in the creation of this book, especially the resources team and those who have contributed articles and photographs.

Published by: Altrincham Grammar School for Boys, Marlborough Road, Bowdon, Altrincham, Cheshire WA14 2RS.
Tel: 0161 928 0858. Email: agsbadmin@agsb.co.uk Web: www.agsb.co.uk

Early 19th Century schools were largely run by the Church of England; towards the end of the century the government took control. In 1880 the leaving age was 10, in 1899 it was raised to 12 and by 1948 it had risen to 15.

"We believe that, if the country is to have leaders, they must be people who have given time to education and had greater opportunities than their fellow men. With knowledge comes the exercising of wisdom."

Acknowledgements: Many sources have been used to compile this 100 year history. Much of the first 50 years has been taken from copies of the School Magazine and this text is identified by italics. The histories written by Norman Dore and Roy Coleman have been used, together with letters, records and memories from Old Boys and the publication *Cheshire Life*. Thanks must go to staff, both past and present, and to the committee for their support.

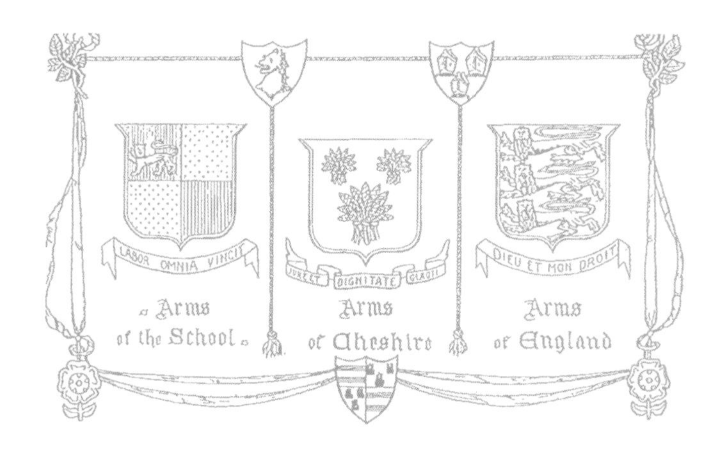

Contents

Find your place in history

6 The Head Master
8 All the Head Masters
12 The Centenary Clock

The First 50 Years

16 The Grand Opening
18 Grounds for Success
30 3rd Altrincham Scout Troop
32 Clubs & Societies
36 Drama & Music
38 Ronald Gow 1897-1993
40 Sports & Games
42 Trips & Excursions
44 Memories & Musings
48 Find Your Place In History

The Last 50 Years

54 50 Years to Celebrate
56 Grounds for Success
62 Cheshire Life Article
64 Clubs & Societies
68 3rd Altrincham Scout Troop
70 Drama & Music
74 Sports & Games
80 Trips & Excursions
84 Art
86 Design & Technology
88 From Boys to Men
90 And Finally...
92 School of 2012
98 Staff of 2012
102 Head Boys

2003-

It is such an honour to have been invited to write a preface for *Making History* – the story (so far) of Altrincham Grammar School for Boys (AGSB).

Our Centenary plans have been in the making for some time now. When the Centenary Committee (which comprises Teachers, Old Boys, Support Staff, Old Altrinchamians and Governors) first met it was decided that we should produce a book to mark the Centenary. The question was, what sort of book? There are already two academic histories of AGSB – the first, written by former Head of History Norman Dore, was published in 1962 and the second was written by Deputy Head Roy Coleman to mark the Millennium. We felt, therefore, that another book of that type would be inappropriate at this time, so instead the idea of a 'coffee table' style publication emerged – a book which contains clippings from the School Magazine, memories from Old Altrinchamians, a lively commentary and lots of photographs from our extensive, though somewhat random, archive.

I recommend this book to you as one not necessarily to read through from cover to cover but to dip into. It tells the story of AGSB chronologically but within that spine there are lots of interesting themes such as sports, music and drama, school trips and much more. These themes show both change and continuity across the years – change in that over 100 years horizons and ambitions have widened but continuity because boys' enthusiasm for their school days and especially the extra-curricular life of the School remains as strong now as it ever did.

As a school, AGSB is by no means unique and so within these pages you will also discover threads of a wider social history showing how education and society have developed over the past century, as reflected in the achievements and struggles of this School.

I would like to thank Ginny Murray and Deborah Nicholl-Timmins for realising this project. They agreed to take it on not knowing what a huge task it would become. They should be very proud of what they have achieved as author and designer of the book. *Making History* is a wonderful contribution not only to our Centenary celebrations but also to the history of AGSB.

I hope you all enjoy it.

Mr T. Gartside

Head Master

The Head Master

The Centenary Committee

Ann Balfour
Charlotte Batra
Nick Evans
Tim Gartside
Euan Gilchrist
Glenys Lambie
Astrid Lavin
Dylan Lees
Ginny Murray
Kevin Pearson
Steve Perrett:
and Duncan Battman (absent for photo)

1912-33
Mr Laver

1933-50
Mr Hamblin

1950-70
Mr Crowther

1970-87
Mr Bickers

1987-93
Mr Nodding

1993-97
Mr Purvis

1997-2002
Mr Wheeldon

2003 -
Mr Gartside

The first Head -

All the Head Masters

1912-33 Mr Laver

Mr Laver had a first class classical tripos from St. John's, Cambridge. He was a man born to lead, with a strong sense of justice and an ability to sift out the truth. He treated every boy with respect; no-one could ever accuse him of being unfair or too busy to talk to a pupil.

At his first staff meeting, Mr Laver laid down that, above all, he wanted this to be a happy school. For its success he worked hard to develop a sense of personal responsibility among the older boys, a feeling of trust and a belief in self discipline. At his second Speech Day he said that:"*almost the sole purpose of a school is moulding character and developing intellect. Character is a higher thing than learning; a boy should leave school honourable and upright with noble ideals.*"

1933-50 Mr Hamblin

Mr Hamblin was a man of great imagination and foresight. He piloted the School through the difficult war years in a brilliant and distinguished manner, never allowing the individual needs of a pupil to be submerged in the turmoil of this time.

The length and quality of service Mr Hamblin gave the School were astonishing. In 1934 he mentioned two features the School was proud of; one was the number of Old Boys at universities, and the other was the newly formed careers advice: "*no boy desiring immediate employment who has left the School within the past two years is without a post.*" He wrote: "*There was brilliant sunshine on the day our school opened and the hope was expressed that the brightness would be a symbol of the light of learning.*"

1950-70 Mr Crowther

Mr Crowther was one of those quiet men whom it is reassuring to find in charge of tomorrow's citizens. He was a kind and serious Head Master, a real professional, dedicated, supportive and hard working. He was driven by a deep sense of duty and loyalty, with a strong belief in good discipline and academic achievement.

He developed the department which taught boys metalwork, and machine and engineering drawing. This was followed by two years of building development known today as the Technology Block.

He believed in a rich, varied environment in which boys would flourish. Mr Crowther could look back with pride on a full life, influential and innovative, with a total dedication to every aspect of school life.

1973: "*We are born only to be men. We shall do enough if we form ourselves into good ones. It is therefore our business to cultivate every sort of generous and honest feeling that belongs to our nature.*" B. Bickers

1970-87 Mr Bickers

Mr Bickers nurtured and enhanced the best traditions of the School, at the same time fostering new ideas such as the introduction of computer technology. He helped win for us a whole host of extras, such as the school minibus and he served with energy and commitment in numerous capacities.

Mr Bickers' quality of leadership and good relations with staff – his readiness to consult with them and the trust they had in him meant that for many it was his approachability which was one of his greatest virtues. An Old Boy wrote to him: "*The family atmosphere you worked so hard to create was a resounding success. You achieved a balance between discipline and the freedom of the individual which is crucial in maintaining friendly relations between boys and staff.*"

1987-93 Mr Nodding

When he retired, Mr Nodding had served the School for just half of its existence; no-one made a bigger contribution to the ethos and wellbeing of the School. He was the best of teachers and his results in classics examinations have never been equalled.

He had a great sense of humour and of fair play. He was a committed and competent Head Master and he led by example. He had the happy knack of getting the best out of both boys and staff. The School did extremely well under Keith Nodding and when he was made Head Master, the sense of relief was tangible. He invigorated the Library and the Music and IT departments and as a direct result of his unstinting work the school was a vibrant place, despite the doubts about its future.

1993-97 Mr Purvis

Mr Purvis was appointed on the firm Trafford promise of a massive development programme. He had to battle with increasing bureaucracy on all sides once this great development plan had been rescinded. Neither did he give up when London withdrew its generous grants. Luckily he was adept at balancing the books so our improved Grant Maintained budget was put to good use.

He was an excellent manager and a prudent steward. When our first Ofsted inspection was promised Bryan Purvis confidently encouraged staff to be themselves, certain in the knowledge that the School was good. He consistently demonstrated his vision in moving the School forward. His firm Christian beliefs set a clear tone for the whole school.

"Without the range of activities available the boys' education would be much the poorer. I am convinced we are providing citizens of the future who are good representatives of all we stand for." D. Wheeldon

All the Head Masters

1997-02 Mr Wheeldon

When Mr Wheeldon joined the School our Grant Maintained status had reached a point when the time was right for further expansion. For the first time in 40 years we had new buildings: new kitchens and a canteen, nine new classrooms, an art room, science laboratories and office space.

Mr Wheeldon marketed the School well. He raised the profile of AGSB with a memorable Millennium Concert at the Bridgewater Hall. He drove the School through a whole raft of leadership initiatives, and we acquitted ourselves well through another Ofsted inspection.

Mr Wheeldon left us to face a secure and optimistic future, with the School going from strength to strength.

2003- Mr Gartside

Mr Gartside became Head Master in 2003, determined to continue the School's reputation for providing academic teaching and a wide range of extra-curricular activities within a disciplined environment.

His arrival coincided with the School's achievement of Language College Specialist Status, which led to two British Council International Awards for language and international work. He has seen one of the busiest periods in the School's history for building expansion with a new Design & Technology Block, Sixth Form Centre, Maths Block, The Grammar, and recently new rooms for art and food technology.

Two successful Ofsted inspections and improving GCSE and A level results have elevated the School's position and established it as one of the best boys' state schools in the country. With Mr Gartside's encouragement Music and English departments have produced high quality successful concerts and productions. Mr Gartside now looks forward to the new freedom provided by the School's acquisition of Academy Status in 2011.

The name Big Ben refers to the name of the Bell, not the clock itself. Greenwich Mean Time is taken from the clock on the wall by the Royal Greenwich Observatory.

The largest clock face in England is on the Royal Liver Building in Liverpool. The diameter of this clock is 7.6 metres, the diameter of Big Ben is 6.9 metres.

Time to celebrate 100 years

The School Centenary Clock is a project to commemorate 100 years of the School's existence. The responsibility for designing and manufacturing the clock originally fell solely to Gary Binns, but he wanted to involve pupils in the making. He selected boys from Years 7, 8 and 9 to help him: Tom Bewley, Adam Cooper, Ewan Harris, Tom Markey, Harry Phasey, Morgan Smith and Munetomo Takahashi. The clock design took 110 hours to complete and is based on the French 'skeleton' clock, which allows people to view the inside of the clock while it is working. The idea of the design is to make the clock look as delicate and perfect as possible. It is made out of highly polished brass and blued steel, so that it looks impressive. Every member of the team will be able to pass on his knowledge to future generations in order for the clock to run for at least a further 100 years. The manufacture of the clock took 12 months, then a further 12 months for finishing and mounting. The clock will run for one month before it needs winding, the job being undertaken by one of the pupils on the team.

The final cost of manufacture is about £850, but its finished value is many thousands of pounds. Manufacture of the clock started in January 2010 so as to be completed in time for the centenary celebrations in 2012.

Gary Binns designed the clock and has overseen its creation. Arthur Hasford created and built the wooden casing.

One year = 365.2422 days
8,765.8128 hours
525,948.768 minutes
31,556,926.08 seconds

The Centenary Clock

1912

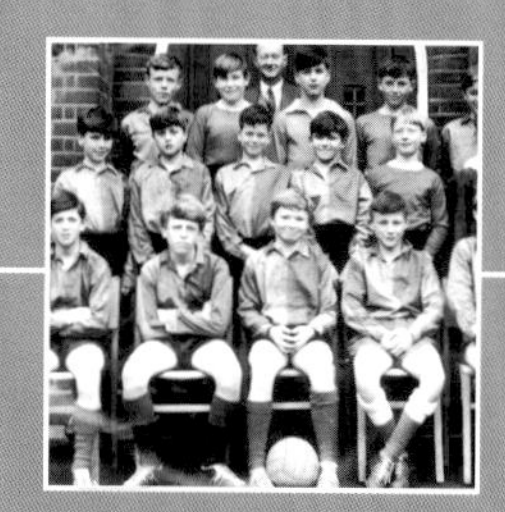

1962

The First 50 Years

When it opened the School had just five teachers and 57 pupils. One hundred years later it has 113 staff and 1,253 pupils.

During the early years the School was heated by a mixture of hot water pipes and open fires.

1912

By the end of the 19th Century it was realised that children of all classes should be educated. Voluntary schools only catered for about half the nation's children; school boards had to provide education for children from five to thirteen. Elementary education became compulsory and free, but in some areas provision was poor. In 1902 Lord Balfour, knowing that an educated workforce was vital in maintaining Britain's position at the forefront of technical development, introduced a new Education Act which gave LEAs powers to establish new secondary schools, hence Altrincham County High School for Boys (ACHS) was born. There had for some time been a need for such a school. Over the previous fifty years Altrincham changed from a modest market town to a busy industrial and shopping centre, Bowdon from a church with a huddle of cottages at its foot, and Hale from a land of farms and hamlets to thriving residential suburbs. The population had risen from 5,000 to 30,000, and no grammar school had been established in the area. The railway line linking nearby towns provided another reason for a school here, since boys from Timperley, Sale and Knutsford needed a reliable means of transport into school. The Earl of Stamford, (who lived at Dunham Hall) gave the grounds of ACHS to the people of Altrincham *"for the purposes of Education."* Marlborough Road had to be constructed first and the County High School for Boys opened in 1912. Saturday April 27th 1912 was an auspicious day from the educational standpoint. Sir Alfred Hopkinson, Vice Chancellor of the University of Manchester performed the opening ceremony for a school that was considered suitable for the furtherance of secondary education. Lessons started at the beginning of the following Summer Term.

How the School looked when it opened.

County High School for Boys,
MARLBOROUGH ROAD,
BOWDON.

OPENING CEREMONY
On Saturday, the 20th April, 1912,
At 3-0 p.m. by
Sir ALFRED HOPKINSON, K.C., B.C.L., LL.D.
(Vice-Chancellor of the Victoria University, Manchester).

His Honour Judge J. K. BRADBURY, M.A.
(Chairman of the Board of Governors) will Preside, and
Dr. HODGSON, C.Ald., J.P.
(Chairman of the County Education Committee) will deliver an Address.

PROGRAMME.
HYMN — "O God, our help in ages past."
PRAYER — The Rev. J. E. Brunskill, M.A., Vicar of St. Peter's Church, Hale.
PRESENTATION OF KEY.
OPENING CEREMONY.
ADDRESS by Dr. W. HODGSON
VOTES OF THANKS
NATIONAL ANTHEM.

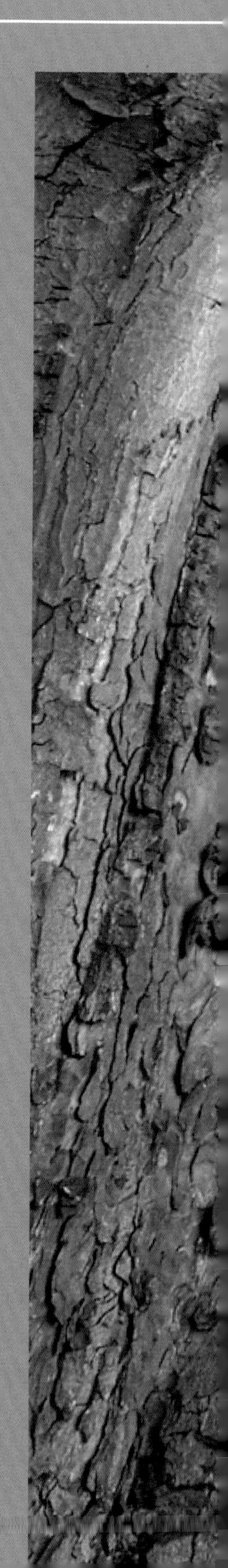

The Grand Opening

In 1070 Hamon de Massey was given the land in this area and for nearly 1,000 years the land was owned by the de Massey family, finally passing to Cheshire County Council in 1910. The School was built and furnished at a cost of £10,600.

In 1912, the same year the school opened, the Titanic took its maiden voyage from Southampton to New York. Out of 2,227 passengers, only 706 survived the collision with the iceberg.

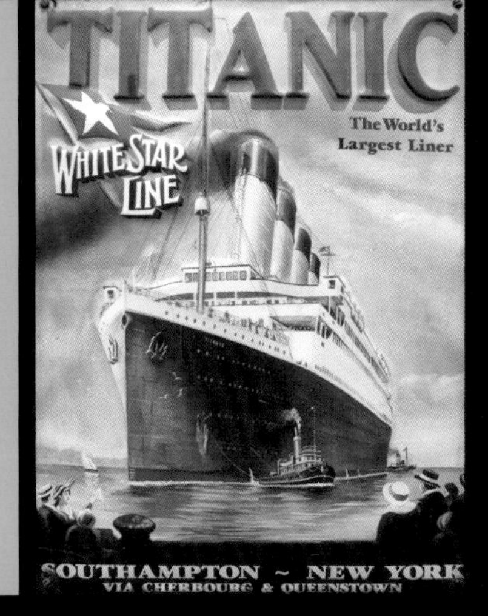

Hale Station at the beginning of the 20th Century.

The School adopted a House System (at that time a novelty in day schools). A healthy rivalry in sports was maintained between the Houses of Gordon, Marlborough and Nelson and as the numbers in the school increased, more Houses were added.

Lord Nelson 1758-1805
Nelson was noted for his ability to inspire and bring out the best in his men. He was courageous and patriotic, with a reputation for having a firm grasp of tactics. He distinguished himself as a naval commander in the battles of St. Vincent, the Nile and Copenhagen. In 1805 he commanded the British fleet in the Battle of Trafalgar. The French were decisively defeated but Nelson was killed in action whilst standing of the deck of his flagship HMS Victory.

Duke of Marlborough 1650-1722
The Duke of Marlborough's career spanned five monarchs. He became a Duke and Commander of the British army during the reign of Queen Anne. He led the army to stunning victories against the French in the War of Spanish Succession at Blenheim, 1705; Ramilies 1706; Oudenarde 1708 and Malplaquet in 1709. Thus he ensured his reputation as one of the greatest British generals and secured fame and fortune for his family – the Churchills.

In 1912 both Scott and Amundsen reached the South Pole, the mathematician Alan Turing was born and Wilbur Wright (pioneer aviator) died.

Grounds for Success

The School was built on land located at the top left of this map, note that Hale Station was then known as Bowdon Station.

1912

The School is well designed with an exterior in Gothic style red brick; the premises are set in the midst of extensive playing fields.

At the time of construction the building was regarded as a triumph for its architect, Mr Beswick, and this was a good example of Cheshire's forward thinking education policy in the early 20th Century.

The School was opened with a silver key which unlocked the south door. The door of the original 1912 building can be found by Reception, just before the steps that lead up to the Head Master's study and the main school office.

Altrincham had become a busy industrial and commercial centre. By the beginning of the 20th Century a railway linked nearby towns making it a convenient centre for boys travelling into school by train, bus, bicycle, or on foot.

The name 'Altrincham' is Saxon and is thought to mean "*the old homestead defended by a ring or fence.*"

General Gordon 1833-1885
Gordon of Khartoum was a British Army Officer famed for his campaigns in China. He received a war medal for his services during the Crimean War, before playing a distinguished role in suppressing the Taiping uprising in China. In the 1870s he mapped the Upper Nile in the Sudan. In 1884 he returned to the Sudan and met his death the next year in Khartoum. In the eyes of the British public he died a Christian martyr.

School Opening Ceremony, taken from the *Guardian*.

As part of the WWI war effort the ACHS caretaker looked after two pigs on the School grounds.

19 of 20 university members serving with the Forces were volunteers. The war was a battle of brains – of chemists, engineers, physicists and doctors.

1914

The First World War descended on the young School and profoundly affected it. At first there was merely the fun of suspecting civilians to be German spies and of a possible invasion, but by the beginning of 1915 reality crept in. Wounded soldiers convalesced in the Ashley Road Church Hospital and staff left to join Kitchener's Volunteer Army. Mr Mee was a Bombing, Intelligence and Observation Officer; he survived the dreadful Somme Offensive, was mentioned in dispatches, and finally he was so seriously wounded that he had to be invalided out. Mr Mason instructed in the Royal Fusiliers and experienced some of the grimmest horrors of winter trench warfare in the Ypres salient before finally moving on to the Italian front.

During the First World War ACHS remained open and boys entertained wounded soldiers. Soldiers at Hale Red Cross Hospital were invited into the School; motor cars were sent round to drive those who could not walk, and all the armchairs and sofas were commandeered. The first of these performances started with 'Henry V', which had a great reception, followed by recitals, musical items and singing. In 1918 another evening's entertainment was planned for wounded soldiers; this time cake, fruit, ginger ale and mince pies were provided. In addition there was an abundant supply of cigarettes! There were performances by the 'Glee Singers', excerpts from 'A Midsummer Night's Dream' and 'Alice in Wonderland', all of which added up to two and a half hours of pleasure.

It was not long before the Old Boys were drawn into the forces. Some twenty of them saw service in the Army, Navy and Air Force. Two Old Boys won Military Medals and three lost their lives. By this time the school was involved; a school platoon was formed, concerts given to wounded soldiers, and part of the field was dug to grow potatoes. Digging was not popular because of the stiff clay (!) but the harrowing which followed provoked great enthusiasm – "*a crowd of boys rushing along at full speed, dragging a solitary harrow and cheering when it made an extra bound over some depression.*"

On one of the Speech Days during the war, the Head Master stated that the aim of the School is two-fold: *to enable a boy to develop his talents and at the same time teach him that these talents should be used both for his own benefit and in the service of his fellowmen. He firmly believed that a boy who does his duty by both these sides of life will do well for himself and become a good citizen.*

1917

The war did not stop the growth of the School. In the Speech Day of 1917 the Head Master reported 176 boys in the School and said it would have been 200 but for the inadequacy of the buildings.

In this same year, the first boy whose secondary education was entirely in the School sat the Cambridge Locals with success. The Literary Society continued to hold packed meetings, with debates on whether the war could be won on the western front, whether the Russian revolution was a blessing or a curse and whether the time was ripe for a League of Nations.

A craze for chess spread so rapidly that players stayed on after school until quite late in the evening and jokes were made that this was all part of the new rationing scheme, as through doing so they were induced to miss their tea!

During the war years staff vacancies caused by teachers joining up were filled by women teachers (at one time there were eight).

Boys volunteered to work in Munitions: "*First we took up positions by the bench and were shown how to file superfluous brass using the vice. A useful if not lofty task but after two hours we were put onto working a serrating machine to cut radial grooves on the face of a metal disc. We also worked a milling machine and bored holes into the legs of machine gun tripods. One factory notice read 'Munition workers are warned of the danger of information reaching the enemy.' We felt we had earned our three pence an hour.*"

There were still two or three large plots of land in the School field, which had to be cultivated to grow potatoes. Despite the heavy soil, the plots were ready for the following year's planting.

The Literary Society debated: "*The construction of a Channel Tunnel would confer great military and commercial advantages to the British Isles.*" One of the objections was that the tunnel was vulnerable to high explosives laid on the bed of the Channel. The motion was lost.

War Years 1914-18

1918

During the war boys undertook a great variety of war-time services; collection of salvage, toys, books, magazines, delivery of Christmas mail and cultivation of allotments. They became Cadets in the Air Training Corps (ATC) and worked in the Civil Defence. The total number of hours worked was 22,720 – equivalent to the work of one man at 50 hours a week for nine years. Total wages earned were £890 and boys assisted on 35 farms, but even so, most of this time did not interfere with lessons. 43 pounds of Rose Hips were collected to donate to the Mobberley Herb Centre.

By 1918 the accommodation problems meant that desperate measures had to be taken. The bicycle shed was roofed and walled and became a classroom. An Army Hut was used as a Sports Pavilion, the library became a classroom, and the secretary had to work in the Head Master's study. She was told to bring her knitting in case there was not sufficient work for her to do!

November 11th

Sirens sounded at 11am on November 11th 1918, when boys and masters abandoned work and flooded out to the flagpole. Amid loud cheering the school captain hoisted the flag to the top of the pole by swarming up it himself.

1918: the excitement of Armistice Day will long be remembered. In those days pigs were kept in a sty behind the Gym. One boy got into serious trouble for harpooning an unfortunate porker with one of the stakes that were used to mark the running track on Sports Day.

The names of those from the School who gave their lives during the two world wars are proudly displayed outside the Coleman Hall.

After WWI the numbers seeking entrance rose so sharply that the School was forced to use the Altrincham YMCA as an overflow.

"We were surprised to hear in Prayers this morning a warning against snowballing the bricklayers who are working on the field. They might, we were told, retaliate with bricks!"

From 1914

Within the first year ACHS had several societies, sports teams, and a variety of extra curricular interests which flourished. The Senior Literacy Society was so successful that a Junior one was formed. There were frequent meetings with talks on the progress of war and the shrapnel shell, but in contrast were readings from 'Pickwick Papers' and a slide show about New Zealand. There were so many offers from members to give talks that volunteers had to take turns at meetings. Members tried public speaking, often without notes.

The Scouts, Scout Choir and Photographic Society were part of the School; chess, football, swimming, athletics, cricket teams played matches from 1912 onwards. Sports Day was held at the end of the first year, and the Fathers' cricket match against the boys ended in a win for the boys.

In December 1913 the first Speech Day was held for 127 boys; in 1914 the Board of Education examined the School, and this warranted a day's holiday. A tuck shop opened – the special demand was for whipped cream walnuts!

After the War

By 1920, the last of the original 57 entrants had left. The School was recognised for its advanced courses in maths and science with a steady stream of university entrants and Honours.

From the magazine: *"Cycling is the perfect pastime. Our machine takes us away quickly, silently and inexpensively and it is time for cycling to be recognised as a pastime suited to everyone."*

In 1922 the Athletic Sports were filmed and shown at the Picture House; the sack race, egg-and-spoon race, pillow fight and tug-of-war were particularly enjoyed. It was well worth nine-pence!

Scout camp provided a life of outdoor freedom, the happiest possible way of spending a holiday. *"A boy is not a Scout until he has been to camp."* School camp at Criccieth had highlights of climbing Snowdon, listening to the gramophone which had travelled with the party, and playing ping-pong.

The Scientific, Music and Literary Societies merged to form the Union Society. There were numerous Science Society outings of an engineering nature such as to the Machine Tools Works at Broadheath.

Four adjoining acres of land were bought – a blessing that the Governors prevented such an eminently suitable piece of land from falling into the hands of a builder. In 1923 the building operations pursued their tedious course and the noise made by builders kept certain forms from falling into a state of lethargy. *"At times a degree of concentration was necessary in order to catch a master's voice above the din of hammers, and which we hope has permanently improved the mental equipment of boys!"*

The original School building.

The beginning of a new term: "*the detention sheet is blank and so are the minds of many! No matter, Jones has a yard of elastic, Brown has a new jack knife, and the waste paper basket, like exercise books, is empty. We shall fill both by the end of term! Eternal youth!*"

Grounds for Success

The original School Hall in 1925, now rooms C1 and C2.

The School Magazine

"In our opinion, the School Magazine serves two purposes. First it is a chronicle of school activities, which we think is the section which will interest boys most in the years to come when the articles will have less appeal. Secondly it provides interesting and humorous reading, and also of a more solid literary nature. In the past this has been lacking and we have tried to change this. A large number of boys taking an active interest in the magazine has a distinctly beneficial effect on the quality of production. After much encouragement, over 1/4 of the School sent in articles and this will inevitably lead to a higher standard of production."

Manchester City News noted: "*One of the best and brightest School Magazines known to me is the journal of the County School for Boys, which is issued at a shilling*." The size, quality and content of the magazine was much admired.

The School Hymn

For its school hymn the School adopted this famous hymn written by J. A. Symonds 1840-1893:

These things shall be; a loftier race
Than e'er the world hath known shall rise,
With flame of freedom in their souls
And light of knowledge in their eyes.

They shall be gentle, brave and strong
To spill no drop of blood, but dare
All that may plant man's lordship firm
On earth and fire and sea and air.

Nation with nation, land with land,
Unarmed shall live as comrades free;
In every heart and brain shall throb
The pulse of one fraternity.

New arts shall bloom of loftier mould,
And mightier music thrill the skies,
And every life shall be a song,
When all the earth is paradise.

Only a school could be built on the Marlborough Road site; when extra land was acquired in 1933 it was on condition that it was used for a Sports Pavilion. Since 1966 the School has owned the land on which it is built.

During WW2 a British plane crashed into Altrincham Park. Many local boys took parts as souvenirs. The Head Master asked any boys involved to return them; they did, resulting in a big pile of parts in the playground.

1930-39

By 1930 the Scouts had existed for 18 years and the 150 boys enrolled represented over one-third of the boys at School. They were given instruction in skills such as first aid, natural history, bridge building, weather-lore, back-woodsmanship and campcraft.

The three Houses were expanded to six; no longer Nelson, Marlborough and Gordon but Bradbury, Chester, Dalton, Massey, Stamford and Tatton - a sign of changing attitudes.

A Speech Day guest noted that *"a striking feature of English schools is the discipline and good manners. Good laws will not make good men, but good men will make good laws."*

Ronald Gow's 'Glittering Sword' was shown at the Altrincham Picture House where the reviews were very complimentary: boys watching the film were transported back to the Middle Ages, with laughter and memories of incidents which occurred during filming. *"It is hard to realise this was not a Hollywood effort, and few would guess it not to be the work of professionals. It had an interesting narrative and dramatic climax."*

The Old Boys produced a play each year. In 1931 the choice was *The Crooked Billet* – a bloodthirsty combination of bombs, pistols, cudgels, knives and bruisers. Fortunately the clever hero triumphed over the suave and unscrupulous master criminal.

The Photography Society encouraged boys to develop and print their own films in the school *darkroom de luxe*, at a cost of four pence per film, instead of using the more expensive chemist shop.

Aerial image of the School.

Later on the School Hall became a library

The 1930s were dominated by the Great Depression and the rise of Hitler's Third Reich. It was also a time of invention. The frozen food process was patented, the electron microscope, polaroid photography and Cat's Eyes invented, the first jet engine was built and the ball point pen was patented by Ladislo Biro.

Grounds for Success

In 1932 there were 445 boys in a school with accommodation for 375, 61 boys had to be refused admission. There were as many as 240 bicycles but only storage provision for 36. The Head Master had almost lost hope of having the building extension scheme allowed.

Five one-act plays about Robin Hood by Ronald Gow were performed; a new Scout Hut, 40ft by 20ft was opened and posts were left for carving as totem poles by the Rovers.

In April 1933 the School participated in an educational Sea Cruise aboard the SS Doric to the Mediterranean and in 1937 boys were invited on another cruise on the Lancastria to Tenerife, Madeira and Casablanca, where they visited the new Arab town, the native headquarters and the Sultan's Palace.

In 1934 over one-third of the School visited London, seeing sights from Westminster Abbey to The Tower. A second trip took in a visit to the Zoo and Croydon Aerodrome.

The Easter Concert included form items and sketches, and Ronald Gow's 'Under the Skull and Bones.' Its unusual cast included Captain Cutlass, Slit-Gizzard Bill and a pirate crew.

The School was one of the first to own a sound projection unit and films were shown every week. Prefects were appointed to look after the interest of each junior form, especially helping with inter-form games.

Altrincham County High School changed its name to Altrincham Grammar School for Boys in 1934.

1937 marked the School's 25th Anniversary; a magnificent new Hall and a Gym were opened in October, and the playing fields were extended. By 1938 there were 465 boys in School; the staff room now had 22 members instead of the original two. In 1939 Cheshire granted permission to form a unit of the Air Defence Cadet Corps, supported by the Air League of the British Empire, a body of men interested in aviation. Cadets must "*train themselves physically and technically for a service which will demand skill and training in specialised ways.*"

A handicraft lesson in 1925

The Government said: "*the first duty of schools is to carry on as normally as possible so that the post war era may find its young men with the full mental equipment to face the problems that will inevitably arise.*"

The School's victory celebration in 1945 consisted of holidays on three days and a return to a pre-war Sports Day.

1939

1939 saw the outbreak of War. It was 'business as usual' which led to a suggested replacement motto 'Nitimur in Adversum.'

At the beginning of the Second World War, in September 1939, the School opened with 830 boys. There were many restrictions such as petrol rationing and interruptions including the constant visits to air raid shelters. However, the academic record was maintained, war time concerts entertained, music flourished, and two American teams played a game of baseball on the field. Scout training included commando exercises, a printing press was set up and a publication 'Reveille' was born. The impact of the Second World War was greater because the Old Boys were much more involved.

Sixty-two died for their country in the Second World War as opposed to three in the First World War. Letters from Old Boys serving in the forces to the Old Altrinchamian described the blitz on Coventry, the evacuation of Dunkirk, fighting in Crete, Rangoon and Japan. In many instances the training these boys received during their years at the School stood out and 17 received decorations. A vast amount of war work was done by boys in school, collecting salvage, tending allotments and helping on farms; Mr Hamblin calculated the fantastic number of boy-hours worked – some 30,000 per annum.

During the war, two schools – Newton Heath and Openshawe Technical schools shared the buildings using a double shift system. The sound of sirens were instantly obeyed when boys and masters sought safety.

1941

From senior boys about to leave school: "*We are thankful that our own school days were mostly freer days of peace. There are contemporaries of ours fighting on land sea and air and several Old Boys have already given their lives. We only know that the same spirit will continue to inspire those who follow us.*"

Gardening and agriculture featured prominently during the war. Extensive help was given by the boys to local farmers. Boys also worked 70 small allotments and altogether 30,800 hours was spent working on farms. Boys were excused from school for a week to work on farms in exchange for a fortnight of their summer holiday devoted to similar farming pursuits.

The war salvage campaign produced books, toys and magazines, which were given to needy causes.

1942

The Scouts continued to be active throughout the war. They held their two customary camps, (even though transport became a considerable hurdle) and met up with other troops in the district in joint activities. Concerts were eagerly anticipated and the hall was filled to capacity for all three nights. 'History Without Tears' was a particularly successful revue; *a boy, having trouble with his history homework falls asleep while listening to a dull talk from an eminent historian and was transported back into the past in his dreams. Here he met Julius Caesar, a bevy of beautiful ladies working on the Bayeux Tapestry, listened to a description of the Battle of Hastings, met with King John as he signed the Magna Carta and finally became embroiled in the Shakespeare – Bacon controversy.* History was brought up to date with a session of the 'Brains Rust'.

A number of boys collected nettles, but the rumour that they were going to brew beer was unfounded; nettle leaves were urgently required for the manufacture of paper.

1943

Visits were still possible: boys went to the Opera House for music and drama, they attended a course on 'The United Nations', they heard a talk given to the science society on 'Atoms and Electrons', and the Music Society continued to interest boys in all aspects of music. The Head Master reminded boys that "*1943 was likely to prove more bitter than any of the preceding war years and they should regard their standards and service as milestones on a long road of endeavour*".

Peace meant the release of prisoners of war, including a number of Old Altrinchamians. "*We rejoice at their return, but there has been great sacrifice. Fifty-five Old Alts gave their lives, seven are still missing. We pause to pay honour to our brothers, and remember the loved ones they have left behind*."

War Years 1939-45

1944

"*The organisation and cooperation of the School are in good hands,*" the Head Master reported. "*The majority of the School are loyal and unselfish. The foundation of this School is rock solid.*"

A letter back from overseas read: "*I imagine the magazines addressed to me are possibly the only ones ever delivered by parachute! I have had the last four issues delivered this way!*"

1945

On 17th October 1945, when hostilities were over, the Head Master Mr Hamblin diverted Field Marshall Lord Montgomery from his schedule so he could spend a few minutes chatting to masters and boys. The Head Master was proud of the war work undertaken by his boys and he wanted to share this impressive record with Montgomery.

"*More than 500 boys, you say?*" grunted the Field Marshall. "*Are they all good boys?*" "*Yes sir, all of them,*" replied Mr Hamblin, and the great man drove off amid cheering. *No-one present on that memorable and exuberant occasion will easily forget the generous compliment so genially paid by so great a soldier and gentleman. What gratification every boy felt at being publicly acclaimed a "good boy!"*

A spirited effort was made to keep life as normal as possible, despite the fact that nearly one-tenth of school time was lost through air raids and black-outs. There was still enthusiasm for football, swimming and athletics; even exam results did not suffer, and if a boy secured the offer of a university place, funds were made available. Music flourished with both Scouts and the ATC putting on concerts. Representatives of Newton Heath and Openshawe Technical Schools presented AGSB with a magnificent trophy in memory of their stay during the early part of the war. Old Boys served in 15 different countries and Mr. Hamblin paid tribute to the 72 Old Boys who had fallen during the War.

Field Marshall Lord Montgomery and Head Master Mr Hamblin at the School.

During the School's early years, a speaker said that this was one of the best schools in Cheshire. The boys were not impressed; it was no compliment in the eyes of the boys who believed it to be one of the best in England!

The Head Master's Office is the only room with a specific purpose to have retained its original function since the opening of the School in 1912.

'Labor Omnia Vincit' – a noble sentiment, expressing the greatness of human industry. When applied to academic study, it implies that education aims to develop one's strength of mind through endeavour. 'Labor' signifies industry, a willingness to do one's best. In athletics it expresses true sportsmanship, an eagerness to undertake training towards a definite goal. We must accept our weaknesses but are willing to try to overcome them with 'labor'. The quintessence of the motto is summed up in 'The Mikado': *"A man might try."*

1945-54

The School was eager to undertake its share in the task of constructing a better world. Masters returned from the forces to teach the 500 boys in school and Mr Hamblin said he was *"privileged to work with such a great team of masters."*

By 1947 the school was larger than ever, and the sixth form expanded to 100 boys. A radio society, discussion groups, cinema club, visits, the annual concerts and Gilbert and Sullivan provided extra curricular activities. 2,000 people witnessed a colourful production of 'Ruddigore'. The harsh winter of 1947 played havoc with after school activities because of the difficulty of keeping school warm and games were also curtailed because of frost and snow.

"In this school there is a spirit which in some ways is unique. A boy's character is given the opportunity to develop in a way that will yield him the greatest happiness." The Speech Day guest doubted whether any school in the country could have more reason to be proud of its year's work or have achieved better results. In 1948 Mr Hamblin reported: *"There are 750 State Scholarships awarded in the country, an average of one to every two or three schools; we gained six. One in ten grammar schools had Oxbridge success; we had three scholarships. We gained seven out of twenty-two county scholarships, which was nearly one third of the total for the county."*

School camp was described as 1,209,600 seconds of pleasure. *"The more school camps I attend, and I have not missed one for 22 years, the more I am convinced that each one is better then the one before."* There were 146 boys, 50 Old Boys, 14 masters camping for three weeks at Ladram Bay in 1948. Activities included football, swimming, photography, table tennis and trips to nearby towns.

As the School grew, so did the magazine; the maximum size was in 1933 when one issue contained 104 pages, although during and after the war due to paper shortages it had to be reduced in size. The magazine has always revealed the same active, energetic spirit which has made the School a miniature community; it is more than a chronicle of events because it reflects the inner life of the School.

At Christmas in 1949, the majority of Sixth Formers turned up at the GPO to help with Christmas mail. Ingenuity was the keynote and such was the impression on the public that one resident wrote to congratulate the GPO on displaying such efficiency!

In 1950 Mr Hamblin remarked that, *"although we have now seen half the twentieth century, the spirit, character and personality of the School remain undeniably the same. We hope that, however much education may have changed by the year 2000, AGSB will still be an integral part of its locality."* When Mr Hamblin retired he asked that boys provide a film projector for the School; after all, the School had been pioneers in the use of cinema in schools. This meant that a more ambitious programme of films could be shown.

1953 was Coronation Year: *there is a definite parallel between the history of the School and that of the country at the same time. The school was opened in 1912 when the reign of George V was less than two years old. Since then, as the country has lived through two great and eventful reigns and is now embarking on a third, so has the school seen the 'reigns' of Mr Laver and Mr Hamblin come and go, and has recently entered a third phase of its history under Mr Crowther. While Mr Hamblin's term of office is now over, he is, unlike our monarchs, very far from dead and gone.*

Grounds for Success

The original stained glass window was destroyed during the war; either by a bomb outside the School or an explosion in the chemistry lab – we aren't sure which! The window was replaced by plain glass, then in 2009 restored through the generosity of Old Boys, the Parents' Association and the School.

Scouting began in 1907 when Baden-Powell held the first camp on Brownsea Island. The Girl Guides were created in 1910. By 2011 the number of Scouts and Guides worldwide numbered well over 41 million.

During 1917, signalling was tested by a Morse Code relay race. The initial message (sent correctly) was"God save the King" but was received by the last man as VOBTASFBUVPOAT
- more practice was needed!

Founded 1913

The 3rd Altrincham Scouts was founded on May 8th 1913 and Dr Stocks was invited by Mr Laver to be the first Scoutmaster. One of their first tasks was to raise money to buy a marquee, tents and kitchen equipment for the Scout camp which was to be held later in the year at Mobberley. This camp was a great success *"except for the disconcerting curiosity of a number of horses who manifested a desire to examine our sleeping quarters closely!"*

The Scouts had their own choir and band which performed in the School concerts and they also formed their own football teams.

The Head Master had faith in Scouting's intrinsic value to the life of the School and by 1914 the troop had 40 members, rising to 60 in the following year.

Some of the party in wildest Wales

3rd Altrincham Troop B.P. Scouts, July 1918

School Scout Hut

GRAND GARDEN FETE

Arranged by the A.C.H.S. Old Boys' Assoc.

IN AID OF

The ALTRINCHAM COUNTY HIGH SCHOOL BOYS' SCOUTS BUILDING FUND.

Special Attractions

Exciting Side Shows, Competitions, Shooting Range, Treasure Hunt, Donkey Rides, Beaux Belles Cabaret, Etc., Etc.

Fruit, Flowers and Vegetable Show ; the produce on sale.

The Altrincham Boro' Prize Band.

Exhibition of Campcraft and Light Weight Tents.

TO BE HELD IN THE SCHOOL GROUNDS

Saturday **12th JULY**

Our FETE is in YOUR hands !

ADMISSION **3d.**

Gates open 2.30 p.m.

TEAS 1/-, 1/3, etc., etc.

Enjoy a Novelty by Visiting

Trappers' Trading Post & Wild West Show

in aid of

The 3rd. Altrincham Scouts Building Fund.

Fri. & Sat., 28th & 29th Nov. 1930,

AT THE ALTRINCHAM COUNTY HIGH SCHOOL

3 p m, to 10 p m,. - - - *ADMISSION* **6d.**

3rd Altrincham Scout Troop

1914-1930

Many Scouts joined the Scout Defence Corps and the Territorial Cadets, doing tireless war work. They had instruction in signalling, ambulance work, first aid and surveying.

In 1922 Mr Hamblin took over as Scoutmaster and soon became dedicated to his task. "*In Scouting we aim at providing youth with the opportunity to develop character and leadership, to overcome obstacles and face set backs with fortitude.*"

In 1927 the Wolf Cub Pack was formed, lasting until 1945.

After the war the Troop realised they needed a Headquarters of their own, but it took 14 years for this to become a reality. In 1930 a stupendous effort was made to raise £500 for the building of the Scout HQ, and this fund-raising event took the form of a Garden Fete and a Trapper's Trading Post. A headline in the local newspaper summed up the event: "*Wild West brought to Altrincham County High School Scouts.*" The proceeds totalled over £915 and the new building was completed in 1934.

The Altrincham County High School Scout Headquarters
BUILDING FUND APPEAL.

May, 1930.

Dear Sir or Madam,

This Troop's work is well known. It is one of the oldest and largest in existence, numbering 150 Scouts, 30 Cubs and 55 Rovers. It has at present no place that it can call its own, and this defect must be remedied if it is to continue to work with efficiency.

It is needless in these days to stress the value of the movement, and this particular troop, apart from its work among its own members, is training officers and workers for the movement in the whole district. Among our old members there are at the present time not less than 14 Scoutmasters and Assistant Scoutmasters, and 24 Instructors.

It is intended to put the Building on the school land and the cost will be upwards of £500. Our efforts to collect this sum will culminate in a BAZAAR and FANCY FAIR to be held on NOVEMBER 28th and 29th, 1930, and we confidently appeal to the friends of the Scout Movement and of the School to help us by donations and offers of help with the Bazaar.

Yours faithfully,

L. Saville Laver

From 1930-62

"*On looking back there are many Scouting events I remember. One challenge involved defending Pigley Stair bridge against the 1st Bowdon troop. Not enough of the enemy broke through, so the honour of the day rested with us. In a return fixture a storm blew up and a flash of lightning damaged a nearby chimney so we called in the holders of the Fireman's Badge to help!*"

The Scouts held a variety of outdoor programmes, particularly ones involving tracking and hunting quarry. They held classes in 21 different topics, and published a magazine '*Trooper*'.

For several years the Scouts held two Christmas parties, one for the Scout Troop, and one for the entertainment of a number of the poorer children of Altrincham, when they organised games and presents. In 1935 there were 150 Scouts, 40 Cubs and 60 Rovers, and Mr Sutcliffe, known as 'Squirrel', took over the troop. He was bounding in energy and ingenuity, and served the troop for 24 years. His successor in 1959 was Mr Killick.

During the war the Air Defence Cadet Corps became the Air Training Corps; its future was seen as a preparation for the ideal of service, and to foster an interest in flying.
"*Nearly 200 cadets from School ATC have joined the flying services and we have helped to ease the burden of their training.*"

Each year a number of Scouts were awarded the King's Scout Badge (later to become the Queen's Scout Award). In 1946 a party of Scouts visited London to take part in a parade of over 1,000 Scouts at Windsor. The King, Queen and the two princesses took the salute, followed by a service and a short address by the Chief Scout.

In 1929 the World Jamboree was held on the Wirral, and in 1957 in Sutton Coalfield to celebrate 50 years of Scouting. The Golden Jubilee in 1963 was marked by carrying out much need improvements to the headquarters.

In the 1840s scientists designed a telegraphic system which made indentations on paper tape when receiving electric currents. Morse Code meant operators could translate indentations into text messages.

When transmitting and receiving apparatus was developed at the end of the 19th Century, it became possible to demonstrate that radio signals could be sent and received and short broadcasts could be made.

Wireless & Radio Telegraph

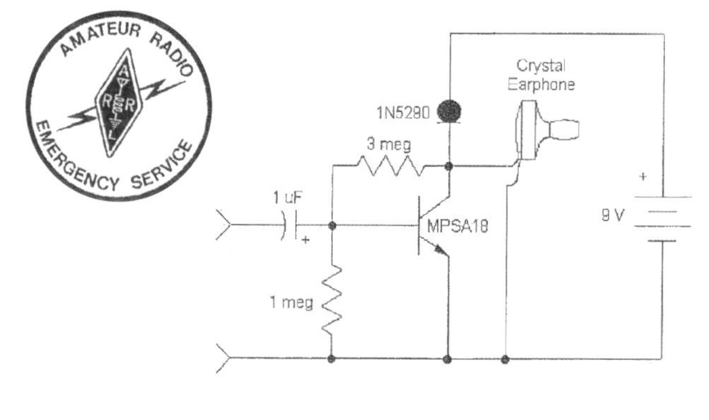

In July 1914, wireless apparatus was erected in the School grounds. A receiving set was nearing completion, and two posts (75ft and 40ft) were in position, the licence had been applied for, and those anxious to read the signals as soon as they were received started practicing the Morse Code.

"You hear no words as in a telephone, but simply a note, broken up into long and short periods as the Morse Code is used. This system has already been used for shipping, saving thousands of lives. We shall soon be able to receive messages from Europe, get weather reports from Cleethorpes and be able to keep the School clock right by having the exact time from Paris."

Radio Telegraph Station number 2JK

By 1921, *"we got the receiving side of our Radio Station in working order so that local shipping and adjacent land stations can clearly be heard. The apparatus built in 1914 has been converted into a long wave receiver and our scope considerably widened. We can now hear from all over England, Paris, Germany, Lisbon and Moscow. 2JK established communication with 2KW (in Sale) and obtaining wonderfully loud signals, despite their crudely constructed apparatus. A valve is still used for reception, although a new crystal set has been tried out. A completed wireless station is never realised; we are continually experimenting, improving transmission and reception – all this is a constant stimulus to us all."*

By 1922 the Station could receive from Bordeaux, considered to be the largest and most powerful station. Classes were given in the making, care and adjustment of the instruments; boys were able to make a wireless set for less than two shillings and sixpence. The Morse class continued to meet because it was thought that telegraphy was still a long way from being supplemented by the spoken word. In 1923, parents, friends and other interested parties visited the School to listen to the messages, especially outside, because the perfect loud speaker has not yet been invented.

By 1923 the wireless craze had gripped the School. A fascinating lecture on Practical Wireless was given to the Union Society. Boys and parents provided headphones for the wireless installation at Altrincham General Hospital. The patients were delighted and found that listening in greatly reduced the boredom of enforced inactivity.

By 1936 a Radio Society had been formed, with lectures and practical sessions when boys could listen to broadcasts from all parts of the world. From the USA there were baseball commentaries, advertisements and dance music; Saturday morning was a good time to listen to Australia. Guatemala Police Force possessed a station, and programmes from Tokyo were found to be most amusing, with music played on weird instruments. The League of Nations felt that broadcasting was a great ambassador of peace.

During the Second World War talks were given on 'Simple Radio Transmitting Apparatus', which indicated just what progress had been made. By 1948 the chief worry was lack of space; it had been hoped to have a radio shack complete with transmitter. All old components were kept and coaxed into performance again, many of these being donated.

The word ‘Radio’ is based on the Latin word ‘to radiate’ as in a beam of light. It can also refer to wheel spokes – hence ‘radius’. The earliest use of radio was maritime, for sending telegraphic messages using Morse Code.

S.O.S.

The apparently well known SOS distress call does not actually stand for ‘Save Our Souls’ after all. The three dots, three dashes, three dots are sent as a single signal without the gaps which would be present if three separate letters were being sent. In its favour, it is easy to remember!

Morse code

A ●▬
B ▬●●●
C ▬●▬●
D ▬●●
E ●
F ●●▬●
G ▬▬●
H ●●●●
I ●●
J ●▬▬▬
K ▬●▬
L ●▬●●
M ▬▬
N ▬●
O ▬▬▬
P ●▬▬●
Q ▬▬●▬
R ●▬●

S ●●●
T ▬
U ●●▬
V ●●●▬
W ●▬▬
X ▬●●▬
Y ▬●▬▬
Z ▬▬●●
0 ▬▬▬▬▬
1 ●▬▬▬▬
2 ●●▬▬▬
3 ●●●▬▬
4 ●●●●▬
5 ●●●●●
6 ▬●●●●
7 ▬▬●●●
8 ▬▬▬●●
9 ▬▬▬▬●

Letter from a wireless operator 1918

“In my opinion wireless is the most important and interesting branch of my work at sea. To sit in the Telegraph Office, to listen to the messages arriving every few minutes and to understand who is working them is a wonderful experience; I even had to deal with five distress calls. Now and again can be heard naval patrols, battleships, mine sweepers, convoys, torpedo boat destroyers and submarines.”

“I was delighted to read of the activities of the Forum which serves to promote any enterprise which the Upper Sixth feel a need for. What catholic taste relishes a visit to the Manchester Guardian and an ice cream factory in the same week? May it be consistent with the desires of the Forum to hold debates as often as possible and the Sixth Form feel the need for public speaking, because it is a melancholy fact that it is rarely the man with something to say who gets a hearing. Many of us never lose the fear of public speaking because we never had an opportunity to speak in public when we were young and uninhibited.”

One of the light hearted debates of the Union Society was *'It is better to be a giraffe with a sore neck than a centipede with chilblains.'* The centipedes had it by a large majority.

The mice breeding club, run by first year boys was very successful; more than 80 mice were produced! In 1913 a Field Club was formed with an aquarium containing roach, carp and perch.

Union Society

The Union Society was very active in the 1920s, before television and film reduced enthusiasm for 'live' entertainment. Its name signified a union of all the separate societies into one single society, so boys might join because of an interest in music, and end up taking part in debates, drama, or scientific outings.

The Society had many excellent lectures on a wide variety of topics, ranging from a talk on *'Lithographs'*, *'Public amusements in ancient Rome'*, *'The origins of well-known sports'*, such as football and cricket, which could be traced back to the days of the cavemen, *'The unusual side of life'*, about aquatic and terraquatic creatures, and *'Life and Customs of the Island of Crete'*.

There were debates on light hearted topics such as *'School was in need of bigger bells'* and *'A tax should be imposed on bicycles'*. The more serious ones included *'All secondary schools should be co-educational'* and *'Parents should be allowed to attend the lectures'*.

The most popular event was the Mock Trial held each year. Some examples of these were:

- *"That our editor was to be tried for the murder of Dr Ali Masulipitanm Razza. He was accused of pushing him down a lift shaft while taking time away from performing an operation to transfuse mental and intellectual faculties."* He was found not guilty through the eloquent plea that his strange behaviour was due to the hypnotism employed while he was operating.
- Another tried to accuse Prisoner Mikimoto of stealing a bomb while in China, returning to England with the purpose of detonating it. He was found not guilty because his twin brother (who had since died) committed the crime.
- One who was found guilty was accused of trying to blow up an Academy using large quantities of pistol caps. These were transported in a grocer's van by exchanging bags of potatoes for barrels of gunpowder.

The AGSB Union Society was inspired by two others. The Cambridge Union Society was founded in 1815 as a Debating Society and was the largest student society in the University. It focussed on public speaking as a forum for discussion and debate. The Oxford Union Society was founded in 1823 as an institution like no other, at a time when the free exchange of ideas was foreign to the restrictive university authorities.

All minutes of meetings were hand written, as was the front cover of the Minute Book.

The Junior Lecture Society showed a great many films. These were sometimes educational about different places around the world, such as the Alps, Himalayas, and the Amazon (geographical); Nelson (historical); and 'From the Ark to the Aquitania' (engineering) or of an industrial nature. There were also lantern lectures at which the lanternists served the Society well.

An article in the *Evening Chronicle* July 1933: "*I have been sent the Coming-of-Age number of 'The Altrinchamian', and having read it, urge all Old Boys to see that they get copies. The first number began with an apologetic editorial pleading that contributors were inexperienced. They reprinted that editorial in the current issue which is now just about as good a School Magazine as I ever hope to see. One article in particular was the stuff of school memories that clearly make this school worthwhile.*"

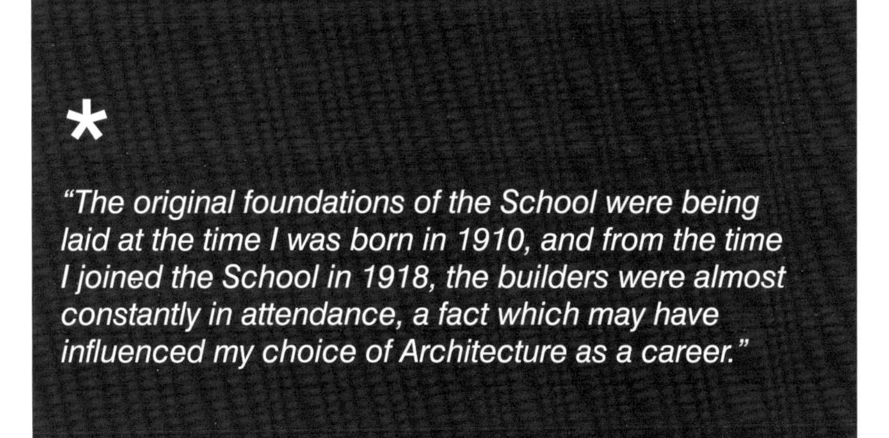

Old Boys

The Association was founded in 1914 for the purpose of promoting good fellowship amongst Old Boys, strengthening the ties between the past and the present and furthering the general interest of the School.

Every member is supplied with the School Magazine. The Annual Subscription to the Association is two shillings and sixpence. There is no tie (outside that which unites members of the same family) so close, no friendship so free as that which exists among men who have grown up together in the same school. Such a tie is worth preserving and tightening, the most effective means to this end is the formation of a live and active Old Boys' Association. Such an association exerts an influence for good not only on the Old Boys themselves but also on the school from which they sprung. As the Old Boys go out into the world it keeps alive in their hearts the spirit of uprightness and good sportsmanship acquired at school. It keeps them in touch with each other, and affords opportunities for mutual help and encouragement.

From the School Magazine:
We invited many well known speakers into School and were privileged to include Captain Amundsen, the Norwegian explorer. He told us about his successful attempt to reach the South Pole, a talk that was accompanied by a series of slides and cinematographic views. He told us how a band of five men and dogs set off on October 20th 1912 on the journey to the Pole. On December 14th, a day of brilliant sunshine, they reached their goal. How we cheered!

Parents' Association

The Association was formed in 1957 with its prime object to work for the benefit of every boy at the School. Its purpose was to obtain funds to provide equipment and facilities not catered for by normal school funds, and to help boys who might otherwise be precluded from travelling or taking part in school activities.

The Association set out to mark the 50th Anniversary of the School by presenting a Sports Pavilion. This was achieved after a great deal of hard work to raise the necessary £3,500. It was officially opened in June 1963 and designed to last through the second 50 years of the School's existence. The Association also provided furnishings for the pavilion, equipment for the gym, musical instruments and a contribution towards a sailing dinghy.

The Parents' Association brought two distinguished lecturers into the School – John Allegro to talk on the Dead Sea Scrolls and Chris Bonnington on Himalayan Mountaineering. Their money-raising ideas were legion, from guinea pig races to a piano smashing competition. The Summer and Christmas Fairs grew in size and scope; a Danish evening, Fashion Show, Wine Tasting and Hoe Down contributed to the Parents' Association's ability to fund field work, improvements to the stage, sound and lighting, and the purchase of a school minibus.

The concert started and finished with rousing Welsh songs. 'Men of Harlech', a military march, describes events during the seven year Siege of Harlech Castle. It was first published in 1794 and it featured in the film 'Zulu'.

"The young always thought the old men were fools, whilst the old men knew the young ones were." Mr Dunkerley, Chairman of Governors

School productions 1920-40

First Concert in 1913

1. Unison Song, 'Men of Harlech', Welsh Air. Forms 1, 11 & 111.
2. Song, 'The Lost Chord', Sullivan, S. Roberts.
3. Unison Song, 'The Angel', Rubinstein, Forms 11 & 111.
4. Song, 'May-Dew', Sterndale-Bennett, A. Smith.
5. Unison Song, 'The Mermaid', Old English.
   Soloists: C. Featherstone, G. Tripp. Form 11.
6. Unison Song, 'The Torpedo and the Whale', Aubran.
   Forms 11 & 111.
7. Solo and Chorus, 'Vive la Compagnie', Soloist: A. Smith,
   Chorus: Forms 11 & 111.
8. Unison Song, 'Land of my Fathers', Welsh Air. Forms 1, 11 & 111.

Christmas Concert 1950

The Concert included ballads, arias, chamber music, orchestral items.

March 'Scio'	Handel
Two string pieces:	
(a) 'Adagio'	Bach
(b) 'Serenade in F Major'	Haydn
Songs:	
(a) 'The Gentle Maiden'	arr Somerville
(b) 'The Crusaders'	Schubert
(c) 'Bright is the ring of words'	Vaughan Williams
Violin & Piano:	
'Sonatina in D Major'	Schubert
'Symphony no 101'	Haydn
Interval:	
Ballet Suite 'Cephalus & Procris'	Gretry
Piano Duet 'Liebeslieder Wltzes'	Brahms
'Violin & Piano Sonata'	Handel
Aria 'I know that my Redeemer liveth'	Handel
'Mache Militaire'	Schubert

Concerts and musical evenings started during the School's first year of existence. Annual concerts at Easter and Christmas were performed, with soloists, small choirs and form items. Drama was encouraged and was often included with the concerts and at Speech Days.

Somehow the Easter Concert is the occasion on which keenness for the school finds expression – the conviction that ours is the best school of all comes to us with force.

The Breaking Up Concert in March 1928 gave an opportunity for so many parents and friends to enjoy a programme requiring nearly 150 boys. It was more like a festival, with form items mostly of a dramatic nature. Each form offered a different item; a short story of Thomas Hardy, a charade, an amusing version of a football match, 'The Vengeance of Felix' and a black minstrel troupe in real old-fashioned seaside style. The second half contained a Grand Circus, a Fencing Exhibition and a play 'The Three Bears'. The concluding item was a highwayman play, specially written by Ronald Gow, called 'Higgins'. Highwayman Higgins muffled his horse's hoofs and surrendered a fortune of £6,000 because he wished to raise his profession to the dignity of a fine art. This concert was given on four nights, raising funds for a new cricket pitch, and *"doing much to strengthen the bond of fellowship coming from common endeavour."*

During the 1930s music thrived and took on a larger role within the School. The Gramophone Society was formed, the Orchestra was born and started giving concerts and accompanying assemblies and musicals. A guitar and a recorder group started up; concerts involved most of the School – both staff and boys. Concerts were described as *"triumphs of vitality and youth."*

In 1933 Ronald Gow's 'Gallows Glorious' was performed at the Garrick Theatre, where boys went to watch it. The verdict was *"it captivated the audience – it is a fine play."*

In 1937 the first Orchestral Concert was performed and the following year the orchestra played at Speech Day. The musical concert of 1940 had to be wedged between lesson time and the blackout, but it delighted the School. More ambitious musicals were now being staged such as 'The Beggar's Opera'.

Gilbert & Sullivan wrote 14 comic operas, AGSB performed most of them. They mocked bureaucracy, unqualified people in positions of authority and the establishment in general. Later composers admired and copied their style, even Monty Python owes some of its wit and humour to them.

1940-62

The Easter Concert of 1941 contained items in bewildering diversity – songs, tap dancing, solo instruments and sketches. All this ended with a parade in costume of representatives of various parts of the Empire, culminating in the entry of Britannia to complete the colourful scene. A Musical Club was set up where boys were able to listen to records on the school radiogram. The school hymn was 'The Coming Race' and was sung on Speech Days.

During the war years, concerts and dramatic productions did continue, but after the war these began again in earnest. In 1943 Sheridan's 'The Duenna' was performed. This was set in Seville, and full of tunes and wit. "*We got the impression that the wines of Seville were very potent!*"

In 1945 both 'Trial by Jury' (Gilbert & Sullivan) and 'The Invisible Duke' were performed. The author of the latter play, F. Sladen-Smith, came to school to watch the performance and he was pleased to see that the producer had fully understood the play and had managed to inspire the whole company. Here was real enthusiasm – he felt that this was how school drama ought to be tackled.

The next Gilbert & Sullivan opera was 'HMS Pinafore', rated as "*one of the finest entertainments ever provided on the stage. Perfect team work and timing meant that the songs, dialogue and action fell perfectly into place.*" *The charming and whimsical Buttercup even managed to infuse a certain amount of conviction into a wholly fantastic and impossible situation.*

Further Gilbert & Sullivan operas followed, but drama still had its place. 'Macbeth' was a memorable production, which paved the way for more Shakespeare. "*A beginning has now been made of a Shakespeare school of actors, introducing us all to a great play.*"

'Patience', 'The Mikado', 'The Gondoliers, 'Yeomen of the Guard', 'Pirates of Penzance' and 'Iolanthe' followed in successive years.

In 1960 the School opera was definitely an in-house affair, the words and music being written by two members of staff. 'Gay Bohemia' was about the life and ambitions of artists contrasted with the matter of fact characters from the world of science. The dialogue was extremely witty, the lyrics gently nostalgic, and it played for five nights. The following year it was back to a play, Shaw's 'Caesar and Cleopatra'.

Shakespeare's 'Macbeth'

Macd. "Hail, king! for so thou art. Behold, where stands
The usurper's cursed head."

'The Yeomen of the Guard'

'Pirates of Penzance'

Altrincham County Grammar School for Boys

The School Amateur Opera Society presents

The Mikado

by W. S. Gilbert
and Arthur Sullivan

MARCH 20th - 24th, 1956, at 7-15 p.m.
in the School Hall

By permission of Bridget D'Oyly Carte

Programme
Price 6d.

'Gallows Glorious' was first produced in 1934 at the Altrincham Garrick Theatre, prior to its run in the West End starring James Mason. To commemorate this, 50 years later it was staged as the School play.

1920s Broadway, New York, offered escape from everyday life. It was a hub of shows (many written by Irving Berlin),vaudeville minstrel shows, burlesque, and plays, earning it the nickname of 'Satan's Circus'.

At ACHS

Ronald Gow was one of the 57 boys at the school when it opened in 1912. He was an all round student, a splendid sportsman, who did a variety of things and he did them all well. He was clearly marked out for leadership and from the first lived up to the responsibilities of his position. Most of the honours of school public life came his way – Bradbury prize winner, Football Captain, holder of the Victor Ludorum Cup, Vice Captain of the cricket team, unbeatable in the sprinting races, Prefect, Captain of Gordon House, member of the Literary, Dramatic Societies and Photographic Club. After leaving the School he attended the University of Manchester, served in the Army, then returned as a Teacher of English and History.

Early passion for film

Ronald Gow was popular as a skilful teacher; he made a name for himself through his involvement in school activities, in particular play writing and acting. Gow had become interested in film making before he came to school as a teacher; he had made some family films and, in 1917, one to publicise Altrincham War Hospital Supply Depot at Denzell.

Films at School camp

Gow joined the boys at School Camp during the 1920s and this is where he was able to continue his career in film making. He made several films of camp life with his 35mm film camera. In 1924 the Head Master Mr Laver installed a full sized cinema projector in school, probably the first school in the country to be so equipped. Partly because of this, and because no suitable films existed, Gow turned to the possibility of the school making its own educational films.

During the 1920s there followed a series of films produced and directed by Gow. First was an experimental educational film 'The People of the Axe'. It was made during School Camp in Swanage in 1926, a one reel film illustrative of the life of a cave boy in the Neolithic period. Boys joined in the filming with great enthusiasm; camp life was far from boring! This was followed in 1927 by 'The People of the Lake', which showed the life of the lake dwellers in the Bronze Age, and was filmed during Camp at Westward Ho! These films were both popular and successful. They were included in an Educational Film Library and shown in Geneva, where Gow gave a lecture on the use of film in education. Later they were shown in schools throughout the country by the Historical Association. The results were published in a report: *A Note on the Production of Cinema Films at the Altrincham County High School*.

Countrywide success

By now the outside world had heard of the activities in School. The experience gained in making these films led to something much more ambitious in 1928. 'The Man who Changed his Mind', a Scout propaganda film, was made with the support of Scout Headquarters and included a short sequence showing the Chief Scout, Lord Baden-Powell. A local fire engine from Hale Fire Brigade was used to provide scenes for a fire sequence and extra scenes were shot at Dunham Park. These were shots of deer set against the forest background and afterwards cunningly interwoven into a deer hunt. The film was acquired by Universal Pictures who showed it in over 250 cinemas throughout the country, a gala opening being given to an audience of 1,000 Scouts at the Regal Cinema, London. Sir William Boyd Dawkins was a keen supporter and assistant, paying the School the compliment "*it abounded in mental fresh air*"

The next production was 'The Glittering Sword', filmed at Dartmouth in 1929. Action took place in the Middle Ages, and it was described as a "*film for children with a theme of disarmament.*" The film was again released in the commercial cinema, unique for amateur films, and premiered at the Altrincham Picture Theatre on 29th November 1929. Gow's last film was 'The River Dart' tracing the course of the River Dart from Dartmouth to its source on Dartmoor. Some of these films deteriorated and were lost, but two complete ones are in the National Film Archives.

Productions in School

Five Robin Hood plays (price 9d) were published, produced in School as entertaining episodes in the life of Robin Hood. Two of them started with lusty singing in a tavern and 'Robin goes to Sea' was certainly a break with the Greenwood tradition! When Gow was asked why the tavern keeper was able to read, the ever resourceful author excused himself: "*he is an unfrocked monk who has taken up tavern-keeping for a living.*"

"I have memories of acting in a Gow thriller; it was about a man who invented a robot which attracted the attention of a foreign power. The robot was controlled by an assembly of lamps – very amateur as compared with Dr Who. In the end it turned on the agent of the Foreign Power and strangled him!"

Ronald Gow 1897-1993

Ronald Gow filming *Gallows Glorious*

Final days at the School

The scale of production of Gow's films was remarkable, with large sets being constructed such as the Lake Village for 'The People of the Lake', street scenes, plus many props and costumes. The Daily Express reported that it was hard to realise that 'The Glittering Sword' was not a Hollywood effort. The whole filming operation was a combined effort, Gow having the knack of arousing enthusiasm in the boys, their parents, his colleagues and their wives. During this period, Gow had been active in the professional theatre, writing a number of plays. Two were produced in the West End, and he received national acclaim for his adaptation of 'Love on the Dole'. All this success tempted him away from teaching. In 1933 he left the High School and he became, and remained, a playwright.

Boys from the School watched the production of 'Gallows Glorious' at the Garrick in 1933. *It bit keenly right from the beginning so that the mind was interested and desired to learn more. Each character has a force and personality and the author was cheered loudly by the whole house.*

In 1984 AGSB staged 'Gallows Glorious' in School to mark the 50th Anniversary of the play's first production at the Garrick, and Gow was invited back to his old haunts.

The 1912 Olympics is the only one to have been held in Sweden and was the last to issue solid gold medals. Highlights of the games included:

- Being the first to feature the decathlon, pentathlon and women's diving and swimming.
- Electric timing was introduced in athletics.
- A Japanese marathon runner went missing during a race. He lost consciousness due to the heat and was cared for by a local family. He returned to Japan without telling race officials, so he unofficially completed the race in a time of 54 years 8 months 6 days 8 hours 32 minutes!
- A Greco-Roman wrestling bout lasted 11 hours 40 minutes – the world's longest match.

Football

From the first School magazine:
At the end of our first Football Season we are in a favourable position to take a review of the state of sports in our school. To appreciate fully the success achieved we must keep in mind that it is progress which is admirable and praiseworthy rather than the number of wins. Growing, improving, climbing towards the top – that is real success. It is also measured by the total amount of benefit given, and the total progress made by the whole lot of us. The novices of today are the first-teamers of tomorrow. We can confidently assert that the year has been highly successful because of the excellent progress football has made. We require a little more experience and some "do–or–die" vigour. There is a host of young sportsmen who have taken up the game with enthusiastic energy and who can be seen day by day madly chasing around the playground after anything from a marble upwards. A glorious sporting spirit is developing which loves a clean, hard, vigorous game. Can anyone deny the progress?

Paper Chase

The first Paper Chase was held in 1913. Two hares and 15 boys formed the pack.
"The hares laid a fine trail because the pack found a false scent and ran for a mile without result! Two of the hounds found it more enjoyable to remain in Ashley for tea than to participate in the home run! The winners had run for two hours and it is hoped that runs will be arranged again."

Sports Day 1947

Fathers versus Boys

Cricket match 1921
Whoever first conceived the idea of this annual encounter deserves the gratitude of us all. On this occasion the Fathers won the toss and batted first, but the Boys had decided to show the Fathers how an opposing batting side should be dismissed. It grieves us to have to state that the Fathers were all out long before the Tea Interval – dare we suggest an essay subject "Discuss the psychological connection between Strawberries and Cricket".

The Boys won scoring 160 runs against 75.

Last verse of The Downfall of the Dads
"So raise a cheer that all may hear
For both – I'll tell you why;
The Dads were beaten in the main
By Anno Domini.
They played the game, let's do the same
Else were we awful cads:
And may we play as well as they
When we play 'mongst the 'Dads'."

Athletics 1918

The good weather certainly helped to set up the seven new records which we made. This justifies our pride in the athletic progress of the School, especially as these records compare favourably with other schools. A high jump record of 5ft 2 3/4 inches was a notable performance.

This picture shows a gym display on the School field in 1933

The 1912 Sports Day included pillow fighting! This was done with boys sitting astride a narrow plank, the winner remained on the plank, the loser on the ground. Tug-of-war was also exciting and made even more so as the results were accompanied by a bugle!

1930-1962

The 1931 Spring Term has been noteworthy for the deplorable state of the ground. The excessive rain turned the ground into a mass of liquid mud and it was not fit for matches. But no player spared himself in his attempt to overcome the heavy ground.

An innovation in 1931 was the appointment of a cricket coach. Without hesitation School secured an excellent return and boys profited enormously. Two new practice nets were fully used.

A report about swimming in 1932 described: *lithe bodies cutting swiftly through the pale green water, the announcer's stentorian roars, a flash of bright dresses, enthusiastic applause from the audience – all the sights and sounds so characteristic of this very sporting contest, unmarred by the least hint of the odious prize hunting spirit.*

Many accounts of football in the early years were dominated by consideration of the very soggy pitches caused by poor drainage. These were improved just before the war and games could be more reliably played.

In 1942 chess flourished, the Secretary of the Altrincham Chess League gave a simultaneous display on fifteen boards.

In 1946 a special cricket match was arranged against the Old Boys in which the opposing team was composed entirely of members, serving or recently demobbed of HM Forces. Especially welcome were two men who had spent several years in prison camps.

"Although cross country running is not everybody's choice, it is well within the capacity of every fit senior boy and a challenge to his fitness."

During the 1950s AGSB supported three cricket teams and two junior teams in the summer, three football teams and two junior teams in the winter and a rugby team. Hockey was also played in the winter and, as the team grew more experienced, more fixtures were undertaken.

In 1956 two boys represented the County in the National Sports in Plymouth. One won the pole vault event and the other was awarded a medal for his achievement with the discus.

1959 saw the first Whitsun Cricket tour to Durham, Morpeth and Barnard Castle School. The result was very satisfactory - played 21, won 11, drew 8 and lost 2.

In 1959 the Junior Cricket teams produced cricket to match the glorious summer. There was a feast of runs and the A team topped the 100 on ten occasions. Athletics records were broken: the mile was run in 4 minutes 52.5 seconds; the shot was thrown a distance of 52ft 5 inches; and the hop step and jump achieved 37ft $1\frac{1}{2}$ inches.

In 1960 two boys were chosen to represent Cheshire in the All-England Schools' Championships in Cross Country Running. The enthusiasm of the athletics teams was undiminished by strong opposition. Two boys also gained sixth place in the shot and the 880 yards in the All-England Sports. The record for the mile was reduced to 4 minutes 47 seconds.

Judo is gaining in popularity - the mat has been thumped to good purpose through the year and techniques, rolls and shoulder throws improved with an Orange Belt and Assistant Mat Master amongst the enthusiasts.

Comments on players

"*A dashing defender who never shirks a tackle and his robust methods are effective.*"

"*A dour defender who kicks strongly, tackles vigorously and plays hard to the last whistle.*"

"*Has played a true captain's part throughout the season, proving a very inspiring leader. He uses his head effectively, pulls up opposing tackles neatly and initiates attacking movements with skill.*"

"*A clever inside forward who rarely wastes the ball, keeping it under control and shooting accurately.*"

"*A forward who can shoot strongly with either foot.*"

"*A scheming forward who dribbles cleverly.*"

Even before WWI there were skiing trips to Switzerland which took place over the Christmas holiday. During the late 1960s such trips were reinstated on an annual basis by the PE department, usually to Europe.

Moscow: "*We joined the solemn opening ceremony at the beginning of the School year when, accompanied by a fanfare, bouquets were presented to the teachers!*"

1912-30

Educational trips out from School were fairly unusual in 1912. Altrincham County High School clearly valued the many visits boys took to local firms. During the pre-war years the scientific expeditions were very varied and several were arranged each year. Boys went to Manchester Docks, where they watched the huge cargo vessels arrive and the vital fire boat, which was capable of throwing out 4,000 gallons of water when needed. They visited Rajah photographic works at Mobberley, situated there because of the clean air, and the electrical works at Broadheath, where boys had to remove their watches because the electricity would affect them. Trips included the Zoological Gardens at Belle Vue and the salt mines near Northwich. Other visits were to Trafford Park saw mills and the electrical machine works at Redditch.

During the 1920s, trips were still local and science based. There were visits to Cary's Spring Works where they made springs for motor cars; wine making and wire weaving works (they made Davy miners lamps); bleaching and dying works; the British Oil Company; the Exide battery factory; glass works and flour mills.

During all these years the Scout camp continued to be the main form of out-of-school activity. By the late 1930s there were well over 100 boys, nearly 40 Old Boys and various staff at each camp. A lorry took the equipment and the advance party to the train, and on one occasion discovered that the luggage van was not large enough and an extra one had to be put on. Camp was summed up as "*one million, two hundred and nine thousand six hundred seconds of pleasure*."

1930-39

During 1933 and 1937, boys enjoyed a very special holiday abroad. These were Scholars' Easter Cruises. In 1933 aboard the S.S. Doric the cruise visited Madeira, Tangiers and Gibraltar, and in 1937 the S.S. Lancastria took pupils to the Azores, North Africa and Gibraltar. On both cruises, the party from Altrincham County High School consisted of 25 boys and Mr Mason. The first three days at sea were spent in different ways, such as deck tennis, swimming, quoits, shuffle board and treasure hunts. In the evening there were films and dancing. Both trips gave the boys a fascinating insight into other cultures and Mediterranean cities.

Nearer to home, popular trips were made each year to the University of Manchester to hear lectures, watch demonstrations, and talk to the lecturers. Topics varied enormously- *The origins of the earth and planets, Freud, Atomic energy* and *Gas turbines* to name but a few.

A sketch of the Lancastria

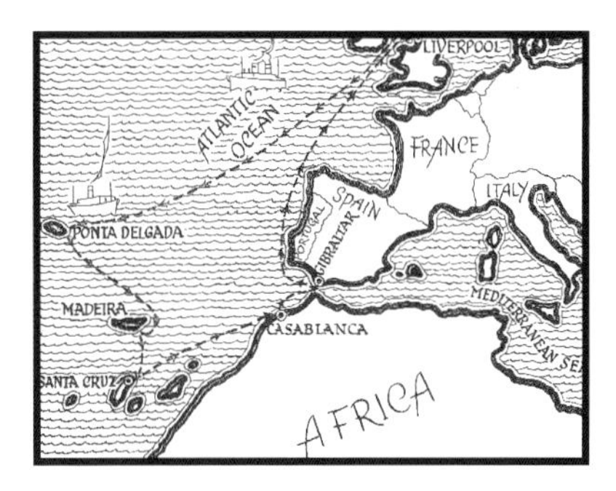

The Boeing 247 was the first modern commercial aeroplane; its first flight was in 1933 and it was developed and improved over the next few years. During the 1930s the introduction of the Boeing 247 and Douglas DC3 made commercial aviation possible, revolutionising the industry.

1945-62

After the war boys journeyed by train to Austria, Munich, Gross Glockner Pass, Zellam See and Saltzberg. "*We noticed the effect of the National Service when a German official marched up and down the platforms, but our overwhelming memories are of the scenery, mountains, glaciers, gorges and waterfalls. We took a ski lift and went swimming and boating.*"

Another trip was to Switzerland, Grindelward and the Trummelbach Falls. "*We took a thrilling chairlift 6,000ft to the summit of Mount Meiderhorn, hired a paddle boat, visited castles and had the Swiss equivalent of our Guy Fawkes Night with a torchlight procession and fireworks.*"

Mount Nielsen

In 1957 a party of 40 fourth form boys took an educational trip on the Manchester Ship Canal. "*We passed the Barton Swing Aqueduct and saw the Bollin trickling majestically into the canal. On the sides of the canal were warehouses with ocean going vessels loading and unloading, oil docks and tankers, railway line bridges, and finally at Birkenhead, warships and a submarine.*"

In 1958 boys visited the scenic narrow-gauge Tal-y-llyn Railway. "*The train was a line of antique wooden boxes to sit on, which we duly did, before speeding our way round tortuous bends, onto a shelf cut into the rock, past the famous eighty foot deep Dolgoch ravine and finally entering the Dolgoch Station. The engine changed ends then set off on its return journey rocking, lurching and creaking alarmingly. A delightful experience!*"

1957 witnessed the first expedition to Norway. "*From Bergen our coach took us over the mountains to Kinsarvik. The mountains were studded with waterfalls towering hundreds of feet above us; we went by steamer to fjords, to a large dam and the hydro electric station. Our female guide was fair haired and blue eyed and could out-walk most of the party! However, reindeer meat was not a good alternative to bacon and eggs!*"

In 1960, 25 English school boys including three from AGSB sailed on the Baltica to Russia. "*Any pretensions we had about knowing even a smattering of the language were soon shattered! We called at Helsinki then on to Leningrad and Moscow; here the turreted Kremlin stood opposite our hotel. Shopping seemed endlessly complicated and time-consuming. First we had to queue to ask the price, queue at the cash desk to receive a chit for the amount then queue again to receive the article. University students discussed their various views and political opinions with perfect frankness. The party organised a football match when we learnt a number of new Russian words!*"

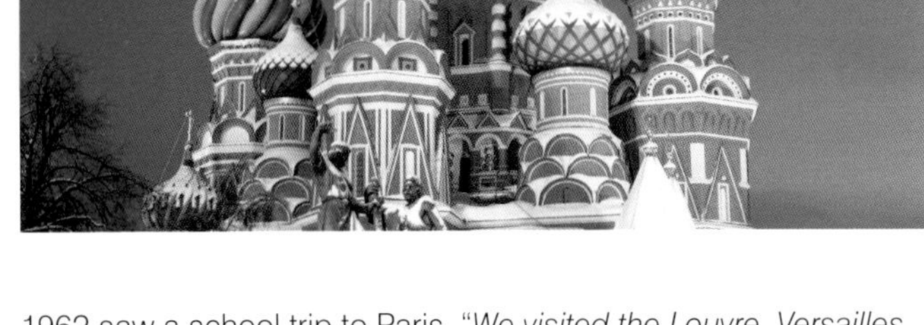
Moscow

1962 saw a school trip to Paris. "*We visited the Louvre, Versailles and all the main attractions of Paris, especially at night in all their floodlit beauty.*"

Paris

So many boys came by bike that they had to reserve the space to lock their bikes up. In 1932 there were 445 boys and 236 bikes, with provision only for 36 bikes.

1914 was the first year drivers had to pass an ability test. The School had a 32-seater Leyland G7 bus, which had a maximum speed of 12 miles per hour.

1912

Memories from Edward Horley:

"My first clear memory of the County High School for Boys is of sitting as a small boy in a field on South Downs Road in the summer of 1912. School games were played there then and Mr Cawood came up and spoke to me, asking me when I was going to join the School of which my brother was already a member. Then came a test (the Entrance Exam) at Easter in 1913, and I was soon one of a happy band of insignificant youngsters whose excitement varied between the old Form 1 room, and a mound of earth in the far left hand corner of the school field, where endless heroic battles were fought.

One vivid memory is of keeping wicket with a pair of gloves so much too big that if I threw the ball back to the bowler one glove went with it.

There was some bullying, chiefly by boys who wished to feel they possessed more power than was the fact. It usually took the form of ordering small boys to do some useless task, such as walking round the school, or half way round the field and back. If the victim refused, some form of torment followed, and I can remember vividly lying gasping on the grass beneath the library window, feeling that my last moment had come.

I think the years spent in the Middle School are the most glorious in the whole of school life. You have been at school long enough to feel thoroughly at home, to feel that you belong; you know everyone in the School above and below you, there is no prospect of any of your friends leaving, and the responsibilities of examinations and prefect-ship are still far distant. To have entered that period of school life with the outbreak of war was a stroke of luck; to the natural excitement and high spirits of boyhood was added a background of constant excitement and significance. We did not realise the horror and sordidness of war, we were children whose toy armies and history books suddenly came to life. I think my generation got the best out of the war at the time, but we have had to pay for it ever since.

I can remember voluble arguments between lessons as to the size of armies; digging for potatoes in the school field, queuing up in the evening for work at the Saver Club, and above all the entertainments to the wounded soldiers. Audience and performers alike entered into the proceedings with the utmost zest and enthusiasm."

Edward Horley

Edward Horley and Ronald Gow shared similar boyish ambitions. In their own schoolboy world they looked forward to a life as cinema operators, press photographers and private detectives, perhaps even time for a little secret service work? They addressed each other as Sherlock or Dracula according to mood. They moved stealthily about the streets of an unsuspecting Edwardian Altrincham with horse carriages and very few motor cars, making back street detours to avoid the enemy or pressing invisibly into doorways to give the slip to foreign spies. On one occasion Ted Horley was pushed right through a pane of glass that cost them one shilling and eleven pence halfpenny each – a serious matter in those days.

When they presented themselves for admission to this new school they were puzzled by a remark the Head Master made. Mr Laver had said the same thing to each of their parents. *"He had an honest face – I shall make him a prefect"*. He made Edward a senior prefect, while Ronald Gow was only a junior, which shows that some faces are more honest than others!

Ted Horley was the first bell ringer and the first boy to leave the School. It is believed that he formed the Old Boys' Association, drew up the rules and voted himself into all the key positions before anyone else was able to join him. This was probably the first indication that he would make an able Town Councillor!

Edward Horley became Mayor of Altrincham. He had always been a fighter and always for unselfish causes. It is on record that when he visited New York, and the fabulous new Roxy Cinema, he told the attendant that it was a disgrace to show white light on the screen between the reels. *"That,"* he declared scornfully, *"could never happen at Altrincham Pictures!"*

Edward Horley was one of the first original 57 pupils in 1912. He died in 1976.

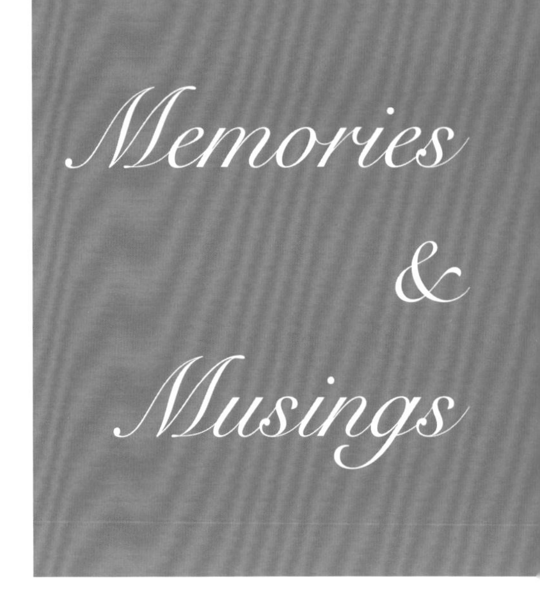

1931

Geoffrey Gough September 1931:

"When the time came to move on to higher education and not having passed a scholarship, my parents paid for me to attend Altrincham County High School. We cycled to Plumley Station daily and then to Hale by train, and home again in the afternoon. What adventurous times these were for the 'train boys'. Every station from Northwich collected one or two boys, including half a dozen from Knutsford. The leader of the pack was the house master's son – a six footer later to become an amateur boxer and police constable. Going in on the morning train, peace reigned as we completed our homework neglected from the previous evening. This encouraged much 'cribbing' so that if one answer was wrong, we all got it wrong! Our best asset was Ken Whalley, later to go to university and achieve a doctorate and become a veterinary surgeon of note. He was a real brain box, but if he got any of our answers wrong he was beaten up on the way home!

The 'train girls' heading for the Girls' High School had a whole reserved coach at the front of the train. This coach was strictly taboo and was supervised by the female train prefects. High spirited mischief was abundant on the homeward journey and the railway staff were immediately alerted when at intermediate stations a compartment door would fly open before the train had stopped moving and a dozen boys would erupt from their compartment and dash up and down the platform into other compartments. We were frequently detained in school after prayers the next day; the Head Master uttered the ominous words "Train boys stay behind after dismissal" and that always meant trouble.

School dinners were avoided by joining the Knutsford train boys who were allowed to go home for lunch which was from 12 noon to 2pm. I was given one old shilling per day to obtain fish and chips at Howard's chip shop on Toft Road. Having one fish between us meant we had money left over to buy sweets. A further advantage to making this journey was that we were not back in class until 2.05pm – always a joy!

I have always been grateful to my parents for the sacrifices they made to give me such a good education, which helped me no end professionally in later life."

Hale Station

Old Boys spanned the globe; in one year there was news from Canada, Pakistan, Australia, Tanganyika, Ceylon, and one of the longest journeys by an Old Boy to the Annual Dinner was from Rhodesia!

I still remember learning by heart the poem Ulysses, by Tennyson. Two lines in particular are: *"How dull it is to pause, to make an end. To rust unburnished, not to shine in use!"*

Ronald Trenbath, Old Boy

The Trenbath family have lived in this area since the 14th Century when they left Cornwall to work here in the salt mines. In the 18th Century the Trenbath children attended Bowdon Grammar School from where they transferred to Bowdon College. Ninety year old Ronald Trenbath started his education at the Prep department in the Girls' School, then joined ACHS at the age of 10. His older brother joined this school when his mother (who was involved in education) talked to Mr Laver and realised that this was a far better environment for her sons. By comparison other schools appeared "stodgy and steeped in old fashioned traditions."

What made it an exceptional school even in those days, was the influence of Mr Laver; his ideas were progressive, revolutionary and all-embracing, and he inspired respect and affection from both scholars and staff. He made it into a school which is remembered affectionately as a fun place, like a large family. Mr Laver employed a champion fencer to teach fencing and wrestling as well as PE. Games in class time were compulsory but outside class time were voluntary, and most boys joined these. Extra art classes were run and boys encouraged to attend, where they were allowed to draw and paint as they wished. Mr Laver had few rules; he believed firmly in self discipline and expected boys to be responsible and "not let the side down". Boys even preferred a thrashing to a severe and disappointed look from the Head Master because they knew they had let themselves down. When a senior pupil arranged that all senior boys come into school wearing 'plus fours', Mr Laver got in touch with the local press and arranged for the boys to be photographed. The Union Society was another revolutionary idea; all the senior boys were addressed as 'Mr', even by the staff.

Another innovation was the 'Social Evening' when parents were invited into school to meet staff (and Old Boys) for an informal chat; this was the forerunner of our Parents Consultation evenings. Ronald Gow's interest in films and the cinema was encouraged when Mr Laver announced he had "a contraption" which he suggested Gow should try out – it was a film projector. School concerts were wonderful events, eagerly awaited, the drama section providing scope for Ronald Gow's talents.

Ronald Trenbath vividly recalled the visit of Lord Baden-Powell, when boys lined up as he walked among them, praising them as a *"fine looking lot"*.

The chairman of Governors, Mr Dunkerley had a great influence on the boys. He was a renowned architect, becoming vice-president of the Royal Institute of British Architects. As a result, through his encouragement, a disproportionate number of boys became architects, many eminent in their field. This included Ronald Trenbath who after taking up art, went on to become a distinguished architect.

Ken Veitch

Ken Veitch is a member of the Old Altrinchamians and reflects: *"In September 1954 I proudly donned my pristine AGSB blazer and cap and caught the 101 bus to my new school. Almost all boys came to school on bikes, and steam trains ran alongside the Donkey Field. Marlborough Road was a mud track whose contours changed with every fall of rain. Crisps with a little blue bag of salt cost 3d in old money from Fred Broome's shop.*

The defining moment of my AGSB career came when I heard the poem 'The Lake of Innisfree' by W B Yeats; I was transported from damp foggy Altrincham to another magical world. I decided that if this was what teachers did, I would become one too, so I did. Looking back I salute teachers whose influence extended beyond the subjects they taught; there were plenty of them and I still feel imbued with their values. We always did our best in Geography, and my French teacher could captivate us for a double period on the subjunctive; we were sorry when the bell sounded the end of his lesson. I gained little from woodwork lessons, but still recall the smell of boiling glue! No school is just about lessons though. I remember the thrill of compiling, stapling and selling the 'Junior Times' and working as a member of the stage staff for the weekly winter film sessions and the dramatic productions. My only claim to sporting fame lay in the AGSB Tiddlywinks Club, which laid the ground for my selection as an England international player. For all that has changed, I keep and value all memories of my time at AGSB.

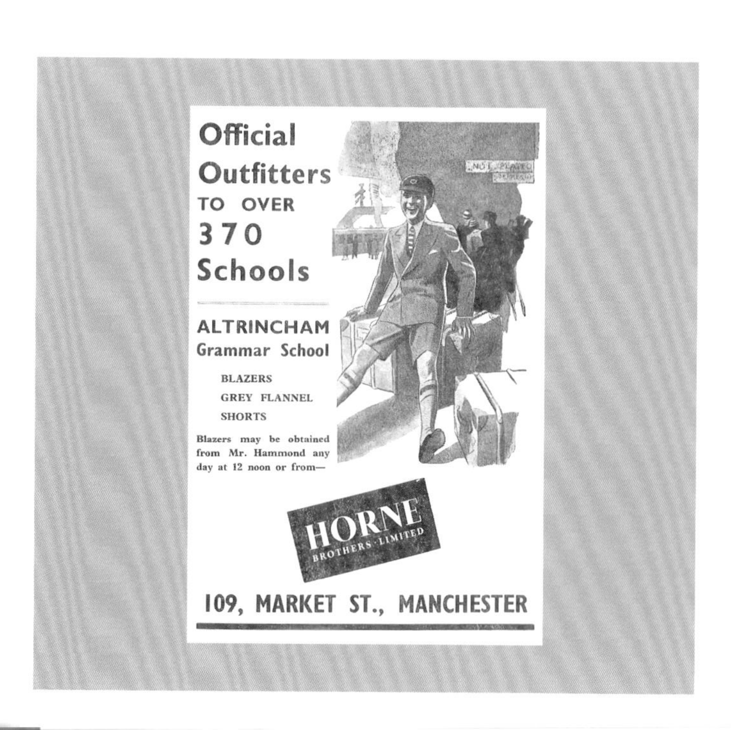

"My first impressions in 1912 were not of strict discipline and austere masters but of ink! I was late and when asked the reason by Mr Laver, I said that I did not know it mattered on the first day. He replied that it always matters. I never forgot that remark."

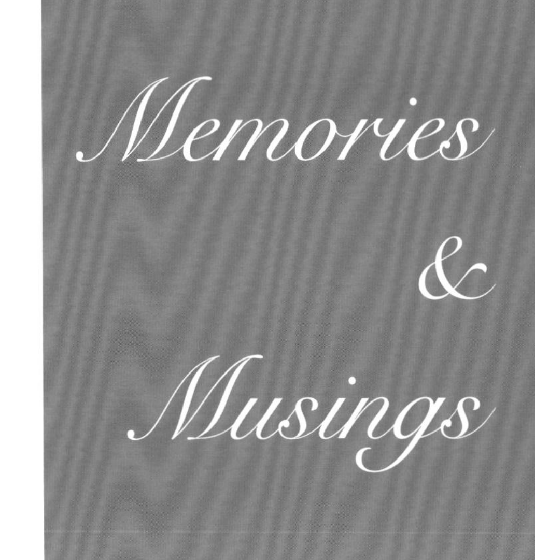

Keith Nodding

Keith Nodding retired after 40 years at the school. He looked back over his life working at the School: *"in the early days all the staff wore gowns and the first and second year boys wore short trousers. Everyone wore the school cap! The House system was crucially important; every boy and staff was attached to one of six Houses and these commanded loyal support and fierce competition, especially at Sports Days (held on Saturday afternoon and attended by parents). Plays were nearly always Gilbert & Sullivan, one of the first year boys singing the female parts. There were no female staff (except kitchen staff, one secretary and the Matron). There were very few cars (probably best because of the bumps and pot holes in Marlborough Road). The warmth and vitality of this school makes it a good place to be. School camp is probably the occasion which most boys will recall; we had wonderful memories of it."*

Pete Pickwell

Pete Pickwell joined the School in 1973 and taught Chemistry. Here he remembers his interview for the post:

"I caught the train from Sheffield and walked to school from Altrincham station, past cherry trees in blossom. The staff room was thick with smoke, from both cigarettes and cigars. The staff wore tweed jackets and there were no female staff. I was called into the Head's study where Bill Bickers had Ghurka knives on the wall. The shortlist of three candidates was reduced to one, which was me; I think the School was pretty desperate! I didn't even get to see the Chemistry department! But, my years here have been very happy ones."

Other memories:

"In 1933 the magazine was given a new front cover, indicating the 'Majority' of the school (21 years). The heraldic lion is taken from the Arms of the Family of de Masci, which have since been used in turn by the town of Altrincham and the School, though with different mottos. The wheat sheaf represents the Old Altrinchamians Association and is taken from the arms of the County Palatine of Chester."

"In the 1950s the School Cinema Club had nearly 200 members. The entertainment films included comedies starring George Formby and westerns starring Hopalong Cassidy; there was a British thriller and a J. Arthur Rank children's film. One very popular film in particular starred two members of staff at Camp, called 'Killer Bloggs of Ladram Bay.'"

"...there were very few cars about, one of the first to appear at school belonged to the Head, Mr Laver – it was a two seater open Jowett. Three of the older boys had motor cycles, but most had bicycles. Originally Forms 1 to 6 were divided into A and B streams, but in 1921 the remove was formed between 4A and 4B."

"Three particular memories stick in my mind; the 1927 trip to north west Spain, the Scout Jamboree and a visit to Oxford. In Spain we slept in tents and hostelries and the total cost for the week was thirteen pounds and ten shillings. The Scout Jamboree in 1929 was to mark the 21st Anniversary of the Scout Movement and was held in Birkenhead. The weather was atrocious – we scraped off the mud and slept on ground sheets on bare ground. In Oxford we punted on the Cherwell."

"I have memories of the buildings – a two storey old building, a single storey new building, a gym, sports pavilion and bike shed. Tacked onto the gym was a two storey building housing the woodwork shop and art room. At one end were cloakrooms and at the other the staff room. Sports were cricket, soccer and athletics. All the staff were very friendly and there were many enjoyable activities for us."

"I owe so much to the extra-mural education afforded by meetings of the Union Society. My secretarial activity in it led to other spells of similar duties at university, in professional life and as secretary to an orchestra. I remember Mr Gow, a teacher who had lost an arm in the war yet still played tennis, and a fine teacher of maths. I owe a lot to my school; I was not good at games but I learnt to swim and I still remember poems I learnt by heart."

In 1944 the Conservative R A Butler changed secondary education in England. He introduced three different types of schools; grammar, secondary technical and secondary modern. The 11 plus exam was devised to allocate pupils to the school best suited to their "aptitude and ability" but in practice few technical schools were established, and the majority of the funding went to the secondary modern schools.

Can you spot anyone you know? Altrincham Grammar School for Boys has many old photographs in its archives but many unfortunately are not dated or named; perhaps you can help us fill in the missing information?

Staff 1925

Prefects 1925

*

One of the oldest schools in the area is Manchester Grammar School, founded in 1515 by Hugh Oldham. It was known as the Manchester Free Grammar School at the time when Manchester was little more than a village and Salford was the larger town.

Football team

Football team 1962-3

Cricket team. Far left: Phil Johnson. Middle Front Row: Reggie Thompson, Ted Mason.

Cricket team. Back right: Alistair Carmichal, Reggie Thompson. Middle right: Pat Knight, Frank Shaw, Gordon Bell. Far Right: Phil Crookes, Roy Armistead, Gwynne Evans, Tony Wardrop, Norman Aniters, Ted Mason, Brian Wallis.

Members of the Cricket team

Hockey team

Hockey team

Between 1920–1940 great scientific discoveries were made at the Cavendish Laboratory, Cambridge. Einstein had published papers which were among the greatest in the history of Physics; he explained that radiation worked by converting mass to energy ($E = mc^2$), followed by his Theory of Relativity. Rutherford worked on radioactive decay, radio waves and the nature of the atom. J. J. Thomson is credited with discovering the electron, and Chadwick the neutron. The work of Heisenberg, Bohr, Pauli, Schrodinger all contributed to what is known as quantum mechanics.

Senior Chemistry 1925

Form photo 1964

*

The first electronic calculating machines, based on Babbage's ideas, were built after WW2. Computers were developed at the University of Manchester; one of the first commercial attempts was 'The Baby' which used just 128 bytes of memory! This was a huge machine using valves, but eventually these were replaced by much smaller transistors.

Physics laboratory 1947

Staff 1973

1962

2012

The Last 50 Years

In 1962 the world stood on the brink of a nuclear war because of the Cuban Missile Crisis. Telstar, the first active communications satellite was launched. Nelson Mandela was jailed in South Africa.

In the 1960s the first working lasers became a reality and were soon being used for medical purposes such as eye surgery, removal of birthmarks, re-opening blocked arteries and sealing blood vessels.

Maths

50 years of Maths to celebrate
The Maths department is unique as there have been fewer Heads of Department than Head Masters. Arnold Gregory covered 1922 to 1963, followed by Allen Chisnall, and from 1988 the department has been led by John Taylor.

In 1963 major changes were seen when 'New Maths' began in the USA. It filtered down from universities into schools in the UK. Local groups sprang up: SMP, MME, and Manchester Maths Group. *A Structural Approach to Mathematics* was published by MMG and the writers included AGSB staff. JMB introduced 'syllabus C' for which we entered candidates for the next 20 years. We had boys taking CSE, Additional Maths and Commercial Maths. The syllabus for the new 'pilot' scheme the pupils are studying today contains large parts of the Commercial Maths syllabus of 40 years ago. Topics taught at university were introduced into A level exams and Statistics became possible when calculators replaced log tables. Many boys stayed for a third year in the Sixth Form to enter for an Open Scholarship to Oxbridge. This period also saw the introduction of the National Maths Challenge which became the Olympiad and then International competition.

At first the Maths department used calculating machines (a marvel of engineering!) and we bought an electronic calculator in 1965 which cost £45. Calculators were used in the 1970s but were not allowed in external exams because of resistance from teachers. Our first personal computer was the 'Commodore Pet'.

Today over 70% of the Sixth Form take Maths. We have embraced new ideas and syllabuses through the years, piloting schemes and collaborating with outside organisations. Our enthusiasm will never die!
J. Taylor

Physics

50 years of Physics to celebrate
Originally the Science labs were above the Head Master's room, hence the bottom half of the walls are tiled. It was here that a technician lost a finger in an explosion!

A new Science Block was built in 1960 with seven Science rooms and an Art room. There was a dark room which was home to the Photographic Club and also a popular Science Society which invited speakers from universities.

There was a scare in 1980 when it was discovered that the new block had been constructed with high alumina cement. Tests were carried out by setting gauges under the roof, but the building was declared safe. The labs were closed again in 1990 for the removal of asbestos which had been there for 30 years. Health & safety rules now dictate that many of the early experiments cannot be carried out, so a more cautious approach has to be taken with all electrical experiments!

The last regular use of chalk in the School ceased in the Physics department in 2003. Today teaching is technologically based with computers, power point presentations and computer based learning (a far cry from the bits of electrical "scrap" salvaged from WW2 and used for Physics practical work until the 1970s).

Two more labs were added in 1990; the old 'hell hole' became a Sixth Form room, then an Art room, and finally a Food Technology room. Throughout the last 50 years the growth of the Science department has more than kept pace with the growth of the School. Science has continued in popularity with ever increasing numbers of students in the Sixth Form bucking the national trend. This growth of the department continues to be a major factor in the strength and success of the School.
A. Birch

I.T.

50 years of I.T. to celebrate
The use of computers in the Science department started in 1980 with a BBC model, a Sinclair ZX81 and a Commodore 64; it was then suggested that boys be taught basic programming as part of General Studies. By 1987 the TVEI initiative meant that the teaching of Electronics and IT could replace programming, and with several BBC Masters there were enough computers to teach a whole class. The woodwork department built the tables (they had to be solid!) and fitted out the room. A few years later Business and Information Studies was introduced at GCSE, using computers to process the business data.

The teaching of IT grew and the old technical drawing room became the dedicated IT and CDT room. Members of department cabled up the computers, and the Parents' Association helped by buying some additional good quality machines.

CDT, IT and Home Economics were then amalgamated into Technology, and subsequently the subject became Design and Technology. By then the BBC computers needed to be replaced by PCs. This entailed installing a full PC network as the start of a school-wide development. In 1993 the School obtained new PCs and a laser printer. Over the next few years the computer network ran spurs out to other departments and more modern cabling enabled the School to introduce the Internet into teaching. It soon became necessary to employ IT technicians, using a store room as a technician working area and a server room. BIS was discontinued, GCSE IT began and A level ICT was introduced. Subsequent years have seen the expansion of the IT network with money filtering in from central government, making a huge difference to what has been achieved across the whole School.
R. Swift

In 1962 an astronomer discovered an object in space which sent out particularly intense radio waves, and which suggested the object was moving away from earth at a speed 1/6 that of light. This was called a Quasi-Stellar Radio source, subsequently known as Quasars.

50 years to Celebrate

English

50 years of English to celebrate
In the early days English teaching was about analysing sentences and clauses into their constituent parts and drawing complex tables of predicates and adverbial clauses. O level composition work on 'Tunnels' and 'The Pleasures of Solitude' hardly set pulses racing. But AGSB was more adventurous in its approach including a time when colleagues disguised as princesses, policemen and robbers burst into a lesson, delivered some cryptic remarks then left; boys had to write an account of what they had seen and heard!

The opening up of English can be traced through the text books which were studied. 'The Golden Treasury of Longer Poems' and 'Country Poems for Town Boys & Girls' were replaced by 'Touchstones' and 'The Curious Incident of the Dog in the Night Time.'

The technological revolution has allowed for much greater interactivity. The daring use of coloured chalk is over and the days of sniffing the master sheets from the old spirit duplicator which could render a boy high or comatose are no longer.

Dramatic performances were coaxed out of the least likely boys who doubtless remember these occasions with nostalgia and affection. But the staff also have memories of what boys have written. "*Macbeth begins the play as a hero, but ends it as a heroine.*" "*We rounded the corner and in front of us was a hump-backed bride.*" "*The teacher is sitting on the desk cross-legged looking like a little Irish lesbian.*" Never missing an opportunity, the English department then teach the meaning of the word 'malapropism'. This seizing of the moment to teach something new characterises the best of English teaching, and will continue in the same way into the next century.
J. Moran

Biology

50 years of Biology to celebrate
I started my Biological education in September 1962 in C8 which was the only Biology laboratory. I was taught by the inspirational Pete Marsch who had taken over as Head of Department in 1960. Eleven years and several qualifications later I was back as a Biology teacher myself in a department of three with Pete and Martin Boyson, who, after a term, left to climb Everest on the ill-fated attempt with Nick Escourt. Shortly afterwards Fred Talbot joined us. We were now in two laboratories with plant and animal rooms in the 'new' 1960's block at the north end.

Pete was an enthusiastic zoologist (less so plant physiologist) so I had to learn that aspect, being a zoology graduate myself; he kept axolotls, clawed toads, cockroaches, stick insects, bees, lizards, pigeons, frogs and rats. Boys walked Rufus the ferret around school, spreading a pungent odour which followed them home. The rats especially were for dissection; this was necessary for the A level practical exam. The knowledge of anatomy, physiology, botany and general biology taught at the time to A level was considerable, the equivalent of current second year degree level, as boys returning from their medical courses would routinely tell us. Along the way we walked the whole Pembrokeshire Coastal path and cruised a significant mileage of England's canal network, partly for natural history and partly for fun. Aren't the two synonymous? Not to mention the annual Sixth Form field-work course – all done in 'holiday' time in those days.

On Fred's departure we were joined by June Williams part time and I took over from Pete Marsch on his retirement in 1986. With the uncertainty over the School's future, the size of the School dropped and we had as few as seven students in the Lower Sixth Form. GCSE replacing O level had already reduced the academic rigour of Sixth Form study and there was less need for our menagerie, although we retained many and acquired Saracen the snake, who was the star of many events. By 1989 things were improving and we employed Margaret Wilkinson and Sue Knowles; before long the Sixth Form entry was up in the forties. Academic achievement was very high indeed so in 1994 we recruited Emyr Thomas and two terms later our invaluable technician, Connie Orford.

This was the era of political meddling in education which was an unnecessary irritation but we managed to evade the worst excesses. The reputation of Biology and Sciences in general was growing year by year as was our intake for separate sciences at GCSE and for A level, so when Karen Crowther took over from Margaret Wilkinson in 1998 we had four full time biologists. I had been appointed head of the Science faculty in 1997 by Bryan Purvis, and was privileged to lead it with the help of the department heads – Howard Taylor (Chemistry), Arthur Birch (Physics), Gill Warboys (Lower school), Kevin Stephen (Geology), and twelve other members of staff (six more than in 1986), making it the largest faculty by far. We even managed to build two new laboratories when our number came up in the game of chance that is government finance.

By the time I left in 2008, we were routinely admitting 70/80 students into Year 12 science courses, and separate sciences were the norm. Building work in 2010/2011 has made life better for the now 19 staff. It is thus undoubtedly a success story and if we find that neutrinos really can exceed the speed of light, and time-travel is possible as a result, then science may yet facilitate a return to those 'science' days past, over the next hundred years.
K. Knowles

In 1969 Apollo 11 was the first spaceflight to land man on the Moon. The mission was commanded by Neil Armstrong. See what you get when you spell Neil A backwards!

In 1966 Norman Dore brought further distinction on himself and the School with the publication of his book on the Civil Wars in Cheshire. He is an acknowledged expert on the period.

1960s

In 1963 the speaker at Speech Day made some startling observations. *More than two-thirds of all the scientists who ever lived are alive today; more than two-thirds of all the scientific progress has been made in the last 30 years, and scientists will double their numbers every 50 years. All our hopes for prosperity in the future depends on what we will spend on the education of our young people.*

The numbers in School settled around 700 boys and 42 masters. Speech Day was followed by an Open Evening when the School was open to visitors – everywhere an impressive display of confident handling of material and machines, films, compositions and projects.

The Magical History Tour

Mr Nodding suggested to the Fourth Form that they produce their own history film of Cheshire. After some discussion and speculation the tour took boys to Beeston Castle, Banbury Church, Nantwich, a Saxon Cross, Little Moreton Hall and Chester. The film had to be cut and edited and a commentary and music were added – the music which was finally chosen was the Beatles 'Magical Mystery Tour.'

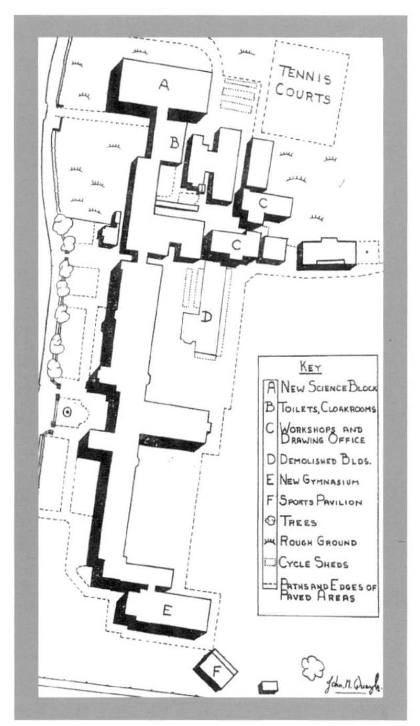

This shows the proposed development plan of the school in 1964.

The School's Jubilee was celebrated with a service at Bowdon Church, a sherry party and a dinner. Norman Dore's 'History of the first 50 years of the School' was published, and 'HMS Pinafore' made a lively contribution to these celebrations.

Some thoughts on the Jubilee year:
"*How much force have the customs and practices of half a century ago had on the present life of the School? We were founded to supply the needs of an area from Sale to Northwich, but the population has expanded and we are now confined to Altrincham, Hale and Bowdon.*"

"*The first 50 years have seen a grammar school education become the opportunity of many instead of the privilege of the few. We started from small beginnings and made our mark by being progressive, receptive to new ideas and willing to exploit new aids such as wireless and films. Enterprise is our watchword; 4,000 Old Altrinchamians are a large factor in maintaining the high esteem in which the School is held.*"

At the service in Bowdon, the bidding prayer summed up the thoughts of everyone: "*We praise Him for all who have guided us, who have contributed to the life of the School, and for all its pupils who have grown in wisdom to serve our nation.*" The Service address was given by the Lord Bishop of Chester. He asked what was the purpose of education and answered by stating "*that it is not merely to teach people to ask questions, but to teach them to ask the right questions.*"

Name: D. Praved

Form: 3L **Term:** Spring 1970

Age: 13 yrs. 9 mths. **Number in Form:** 32 **Average Age:** 14 yrs. 9 mths.

Term Order: 3rd **Examination Order:** 5th

Subject	Term Grade	Place in Exam	No. in Exam	Remarks	Signatures
English	B+	7	32	Still room at the top.	A. D. Verb
History	A	1	32	He is making it.	V. I. King
Geography	E—	31	32	He tells everybody where to go.	I. M. Lost
French	D—	27	32	He has a cute accent.	Sid. C. Diller
Latin	D+	III	xxxii	Hic unus bonus pueri–But he's useless at Latin!	T. O. Gar
Mathematics	B—	14	32	His favourite figures are 36,22,36.	P. Brain
Chemistry	C	17	32	Good with retorts, but work stinks!	L. E. Ment
Physics	B+	11.5	32	He has learnt to swim.	I. N. Stein
Art	C+	15	32	He has had a few brushes with the law.	Constable
Handicraft	B+	13	32	This little chiseller is a chip off the old block.	Chippendale
Scripture	A—	4	32	Often caught praying in class.	A. Theist
Music			32	Another Beethoven; he's deaf.	V. I. O'Lynn
Gym (P.E.)	A+			He has improved in leaps and bounds.	H. E. Mann

Times Absent: 0 **Times Late:** 12 **Detentions:** Lost Count!

Headmaster: He will go far–I hope.

Form Master: He has the ability to do worse.

Humorous School report

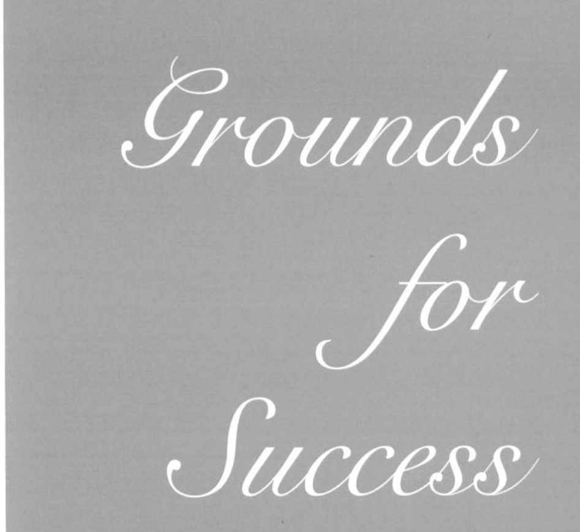

In 1969 a huge machine transplanted the long row of horse chestnut trees which bordered the playing fields on to the boundary with the railway line. This brought the 'Donkey Field' and the rest of the land into use for games.

1970s

In 1970 Mr Bickers succeeded Mr Crowther to become the fourth Head Master of Altrincham Grammar School for Boys.

The School was featured in Cheshire Life as the '*School of the Month*' (see pages 62 and 63). It gave a very agreeable first impression of the School and described it as "*a School to which parents must be profoundly grateful for the kind of education and training in living it offers their sons. The School's academic record, range of activities and the tireless efforts of the staff and vigour of the Parents' Association are impressive.*" The School Magazine was also highly praised.

"*The Maths Department is collecting Green Shield Stamps to accumulate enough to buy an electronic computer. We appeal to you to improve on the 83 books already handed in*." This was soon increased to 108 books and these were exchanged for two electronic calculating machines.

The School's audio visual equipment consisted of six tape recorders, three record players and five film strip and slide projectors. It was intended to supplement this with four overhead projectors, *which might possibly replace the blackboard*. The School also acquired a thermal copier and a recording machine "*which will record a TV programme so we can play it back when required.*"

Fund raising charities continued every year. The School raised money for the NSPCC, the Coronary Care Unit at Wythenshawe, and the Blue Peter Appeal. A new scheme was inaugurated to help senior citizens by assigning teams consisting of an older and a junior boy to visit them and do simple tasks.

What the School looked like in 1976

Few schools had such a wide reaching and invaluable Career Service. From his third year each boy was given several talks on careers, attended career conventions, and received information about university application, apprenticeships, trainees, holiday work and visits to local factories.

By 1976 there were 830 boys in School, and space was at a premium. There were 23 teaching sessions when there were no rooms available and the need for extra Science labs and classrooms was paramount.

Fred Talbot, one of the Science staff, was given his own short programme on Radio Manchester to encourage amateur astronomy.

"*Being Head has frustrations, I seem to spend more time filing circulars and submitting returns than educating our boys. I recently received four pages of detailed instructions on the use of step ladders!*" Mr Bickers

1986: "*If the 75th Anniversary looks assured, reaching the 100th remains doubtful. Whether the shift in political balance after the latest local elections will affect matters remains to be seen.*" Mr Bickers

1980s

Mr Bickers appreciated the need to apply ourselves seriously to Computer Technology. He had to ask the Parents' Association to help; *"at present all we have is a link with a computer at Salford University and we need our own 'mini-computers' for all departments."*

Fred Talbot has made several appearances on Granada Reports, billed as a 'Cosmic Authority' and is now working on a series of his own for Granada. Twenty–five years ago the Space Age really started with the satellite Sputnik 1, but little astronomy education has been taught in schools here in England. Space studies are now normal in America and Russia. So, 20 boys at AGSB have started a one-year course in astronomy with Fred Talbot covering the planets, the structure of the universe and some maths.

A Sixth Former, Onye Igwe, was presented with a Greater Manchester Young Citizen's Award in acknowledgement of the work he did with Youth Clubs. Knighthoods were awarded to two Old Boys, Robert Booth for services to industry and to Geoffrey Wardale, Permanent Secretary at the Ministry of the Environment.

The Chief Constable of Manchester gave an accomplished address on Speech Day. He observed that being a public figure gave you nowhere to hide but this is not a burden. It forces you to stand up for your own values and to be yourself. For everybody, there should be "*no hiding place*"

'Games Workshop' was the brainchild of Ian Livingstone and Steve Jackson. It was launched in a modest way in 1975, operating out of Ian's London flat. In 1976 both gave up their jobs, went to the US and began a long struggle to produce new games. 'Dungeons and Dragons' was not treated seriously until 1977. It is a role-playing game where one player is Dungeon Master guiding the other players into an exotic fantasy games world of magic and monsters. These two ex-pupils have written 15 books which have been translated into 15 languages; in 10 years they have turned a spare time venture into a multi-million international games empire.

The School held its first Open Evening in 1987 for feeder primary schools. The result was an impressive and entertaining series of displays, ranging from an awesome exhibition of weight lifting to a "spectaculum" put on by the Classics department. A prospective new boy wrote that he first imagined a place where teachers paraded around in black robes and mortar boards, with a cane in one hand and a pile of books in the other. However, he soon realised he was mistaken. *"Boys were kind and helpful and teachers humorous and easy going. I loved the keyboards in the music room and the computers, and I shall enjoy my time at AGSB."*

Rufus the ferret died of old age after many years of sterling service helping boys to take an interest in Biology and making them smellier than normal.

Grounds for Success

1990-2000

In 1990 Altrincham celebrated 700 years of the Charter; an AGSB pupil was elected Town Crier and others acted as Squires for the Knight's parade. The successes in that year were wide ranging, one student achieved a place at the Royal Academy of Music; a second an award of an Officer Cadetship at Sandhurst; a Year 12 student won an individual trophy for a special contribution to the Young Enterprise; and a Cup was presented for exceptional results at GCSE. Academic standing was high and the UCAS points score placed AGSB among the top schools in the country. The International Mathematical Olympiad was introduced and Mike Fryers won first a Bronze, then a Gold Medal. A first year pupil was invited to Riga to represent Great Britain's under 14 Chess team in matches against Russia. An ex-pupil was awarded the prestigious Mayhew Prize at Cambridge for the best paper in Applied Mathematics. Both poetry and a script for a short film with Granada TV won prizes. Many new subjects were being introduced, which enabled boys to take an impressive array of subjects at university.

By 1996 the School roll totalled 912 pupils and was still growing. The celebration of Founder's Day was revived and one of the first guest speakers was Paul Watson, an ex-pupil, from the world of television. He recalled that he was never top of the class, nor a prefect, nor a sportsman. Instead he became a documentary film maker! Having passed the 11 plus, he found education at AGSB to be a wonderful and liberating experience which allowed him to grow and make decisions about his life.

The Design and Technology department saw great changes. The Engineering Scheme was designed to expose boys to the world of engineering, and boys were invited to Sellafield to work on a £10 million pound project involving the transfer of nuclear waste. These boys were awarded the CREST Gold Award and registered with the Royal Academy of Engineers.

In 1999 Ofsted decreed that *"the School's strengths far outweighs its weaknesses. In particular boys develop mature attitudes and an active sense of responsibility. The School provides consistently good teaching and a range of extra curricular activities in which boys enthusiastically participate."*

Twelve boys took on the Duke of Edinburgh Award Scheme when it was first introduced, but within a year this number rose to seventy.

A School Council was started in order to give the younger boys a voice in the running of the School.

And finally in 1999 boys involved in Community Service visited Nursing Homes and Brentwood School where they entertained the residents and joined in some very strenuous PE with the youngsters. AGSB adopted the village of Busoga, in Uganda, raising money for a well, and soon afterwards the Bishop of Busoga paid the School a visit.

THE WHITE HOUSE
WASHINGTON

October 1, 1993

Andrew Owen
11 Road
Hale, Altrincham
Cheshire, England WA15-

Dear Andrew:

Thank you for your letter regarding the scheduled execution of Gary Graham.

In state cases such as Gary Graham's, there is no legal basis for the President to intervene to prevent an execution. National involvement in state cases is constrained by our federal system.

Executions raise extremely difficult moral and ethical issues. People who hold sincere and profound beliefs often differ on issues concerning life and death. I have spent countless hours myself contemplating the justifications for the state to take a human life. My own decision to uphold death sentences in Arkansas was reached only after much prayer, study, and consultation.

Thank you very much for writing me with your thoughts.

Sincerely,

Bill Clinton

An Amnesty International group started up and their passionate letters sent round the world resulted in this response from President Clinton.

From 2007 Year 7 have had the opportunity to try rock climbing, abseiling, zip wire and night navigation, during their three day PGL adventure experience in October.

"Preparation for life in the modern world means much more than in 1912. I can no longer just be an educator. I am, in effect, running a business with a turnover of more than three million pounds." D. Wheeldon

'The Grammar'

Freddie Flintoff on the opening day of 'The Grammar'

2000-2012

In 2000 the Stamford Hall was opened, six new classrooms were added and new laboratories were planned for the following year.

On March 27th a Millennium Concert was held at the Bridgewater Hall, celebrating all that is good about the School. 300 boys entertained a capacity audience on a most memorable occasion.

Year 12 boys running Young Enterprise formed three companies 'A Splash of Colour', which produced T-shirts; 'The Firm', which was in the business of making money; and 'Hand Made', which was judged the best Young Enterprise company in Trafford. The following year 'Enigma' won the Trafford Cup for the best Young Enterprise company.

Challenge of Industry was a valuable and enjoyable two days. It showed clearly that pupils had little idea of what takes place in industry, and the boys were shown what to expect and how to deal with it. They had to design soap packages and take part in a meeting of Trade Unions and Shop Stewards. Their final task required them to make prototypes then negotiate for a contract at an agreed price.

In 2003 the School was awarded Specialist School Status as a Language College. It would give languages a higher profile, increase the opportunity to study languages and improve contacts between AGSB and other countries.

The Music department won over £20,000 which went towards buying state of the art music technology equipment and the appointment of Mr Myers as Director of Music meant that the School started to Swing!

A crucial weakness of AGSB was its sports facilities. A number of avenues were explored to secure funding including an abortive plan to sell off some land close to Heath Road. It was in 2006 when everything fell into place. The School secured sponsorship from Peel Holdings and won a £2.8 million government grant. The astroturf was ready for use in 2007 and 'The Grammar' was opened in 2008. On the first day Andrew 'Freddie' Flintoff paid a surprise visit to a whole school assembly in the Peel Hall.

One of our enterprising Year 12 students created the first documentary on the fascinating creatures known as 'teachers'; entitled 'Walking with Teachers.' Risking detention, suspension and expulsion, the film of the life of teachers evolved to illustrate why some teachers are being driven to extinction. See for yourself some of the footage on 'You Tube'!

In 2006 the new Sixth Form Centre was opened. Fourteen Sixth Form students were offered places at Oxbridge, but they still found time to be the mainstay of extra curricular activities.

An Eco-Committee was set up, working towards the Eco Schools award. As part of this the School's carbon footprint was calculated and an action plan written. In 2008 the Eco-Committee was given this acronym:

Always recycle cans, bottles, paper.

Get up; don't drive when you can walk.

Save energy by turning off unused lights.

Be aware and use only the paper you need.

"The success of schools depends on the spirit and character of the senior boys and the example they set to the younger boys. This School is one of the best in the North of England."

World Challenge

World Challenge expeditions are organised by Dr. Marsden. The first World Challenge expedition was launched in 1999. A 31 day trip to Venezuela involved trekking in the Andes, flying in 4-seater planes over the rainforest before travelling up the Orinoco in dugout canoes to Angel Falls, working in a shanty town and relaxing on the coast.

Since then expeditions have been organised every two years, to Vietnam, Peru, South Africa, Ecuador (in 2012 to Argentina). All have taken the same format: acclimatising to the new environment – both climate and culture – then trekking in the mountains, working on a project with a local community, and visits to cultural/historical sights.

"Working within communities in Kwazulu Natal and Vietnam was a real eye-opener. Facilities were basic and families self-sufficient, although they were willing to share what little they had. We spent time renovating community facilities, teaching in local schools and playing with the children. The project in Ecuador, deep in the Amazon, was in a remote community with no electricity or running water and washing was done in the river!

Trekking has often been at altitude, with major treks around Ausangate (Peru, 6,000m) and the toughest yet, reaching the summit of Cotapaxi in Ecuador (5,980m) after using axes and crampons to climb across glaciers and snow-bridges for five hours. Trekking in Vietnam and South Africa was both beautiful and demanding."

Other major features include sailing in the South China Sea, getting to Machu Picchu at dawn, seeing the 'big five' on safari, whale watching, kayaking with hippo and crocodile and white water rafting. By far the most enjoyable part however has been seeing the team develop from a bunch of disparate Year 11 boys to a close-knit team, able to plan accommodation and transport across third-world countries, to camp and cook, to help out in difficult situations and to do all this together, with a smile.

Machu Picchu

Activities Week

Activities Week is now well established at the end of the summer term, when so many boys and staff are out of School on language trips abroad. Boys are able to choose several activities, the choice ranging from sports, intellectual games, fun challenges, learning new skills, voluntary work and a great deal of subject-based fun. Boys make (and fly) a hot air balloon, a fully working radio, an animated cartoon film, a powered Lego vehicle, towers made of straws; they learn how to maintain their bicycle, to improve their photographic skills and how to cook themselves a meal.

"There is African Drumming, Fire Writing, Scrabble, Bridge and games to make us more aware of third world poverty. Every sport is catered for from a visit to the Manchester United Football ground to playing at the JJB, archery, golf, rock climbing, a day's cycling, ice skating, boxing and horse riding.

The final day is for trips out; these are to Paintballing, Chill Factore, the IMAX cinema, Blackpool and the all time favourite, Alton Towers. These days are an excellent way to round off the School year."

Students from Years 7, 8 and 9 enjoy their activities during the final week of summer term.

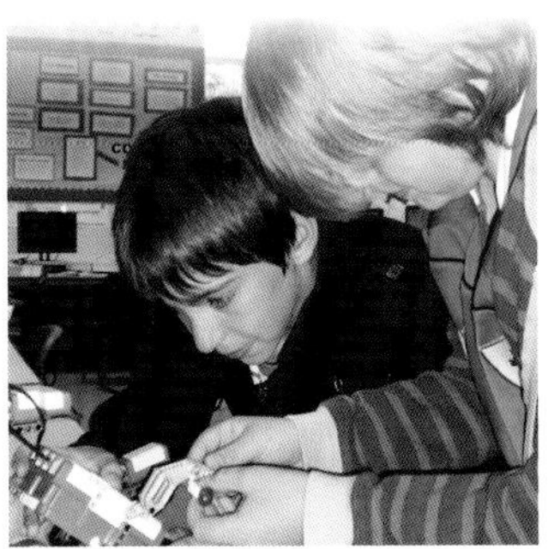

In October 1970 AGSB featured in 'Cheshire Life' as the "*School of the Month*".

In 1970 boys spent a week in Shropshire learning to glide. A gilder was catapulted from the edge of a hill rising to $1^1/_2$ thousand feet. Several boys managed to fly the glider when the instructor handed over controls.

1970

AGSB was featured in *Cheshire Life*.

"There is nothing pretentious about AGSB; instead it is a school to respect, with an intangible something which makes it a school to which parents must be profoundly grateful for the kind of education and training it offers.

The School's academic record is very good, but the aim of the School is to train the boys to live, rather than merely to study, so although every type of academic activity study is encouraged, non-academic pursuits and sports are taken just as seriously.

The Parents' Association is tirelessly cooperative and without which much of the School's extra-curricular activity would be curtailed. It has bought, insured and maintains two minibuses, paid for a cricket pavilion, musical instruments, furnishings for the prefects' room. There is plenty of evidence of in-school activity in drama, chess, public speaking, debating and Student Christian Fellowship. The school magazine is well printed and one which parents as well as pupils can enjoy.

To mark the retirement of Mr Crowther, the school is reverting to Gilbert & Sullivan with a production of 'Pirates of Penzance', which was performed in his first year as Head Master in 1950; this was a well deserved tribute to the quiet man who has given the School such inestimable service."

Boys playing chess

Biology lesson

Head Master and Prefect

Text by kind permission of Catherine Scott of Cheshire Life.
Photographs by kind permission of Cyril Lindley of Cheshire Life.

In October 1970 Alexksandr Solzhenitsyn won the Nobel Prize for Literature, and in Vietnam the worst monsoon to hit the area in six years caused large floods and virtually halted the Vietnam War.

Cheshire Life Article

Learning the art of orienteering

The Scouts

Boys playing football

Biology lesson

Basketball practice

Physics Lesson

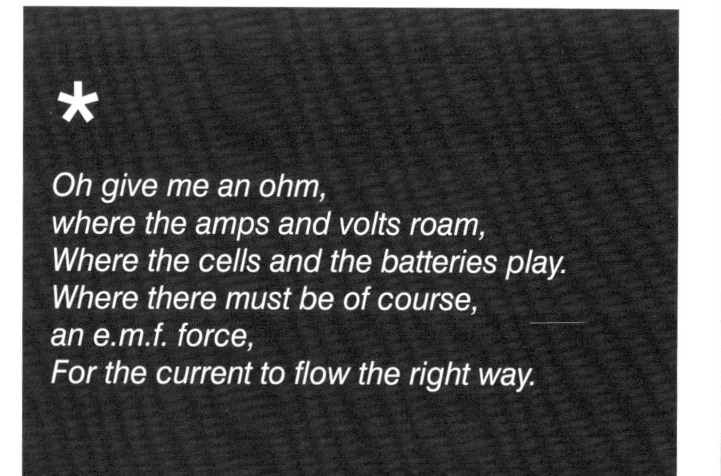

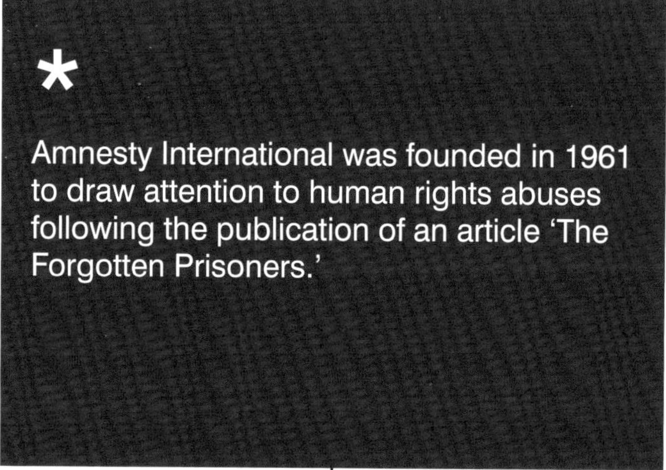

1962-90

Societies flourished during these years and below are some examples.

The Railway Society organised four coach tours to Railway Depots - Carlisle and Scotland, Cumberland, Derby, and Bournemouth. They had rail tours on the 'Waverley Special' and the 'Tudor Minstrel' during which the trains reached top speeds of 88mph.

The Science Society had a full programme of events each year - visiting speakers, trips out to the University of Manchester, lectures and films. The Society took advantage of the Science Fair (which Manchester pioneered) to display three exhibits – small animal skeletons, an oscilloscope and a harmonograph. One particularly interesting visit was to Cheadle Royal, where boys were able to talk to the patients and visit their very successful workshop.

The Debating Society continued its discussions on a range of topics. 'This House believes that women are superior to men' was heavily defeated even though there was an equal number of boys and girls present! Other topics were 'This House believes that man created God, not God man', 'This House believes that flower power is the weed of society', 'This House believes in compulsory arts for scientists and science for artists in the Sixth Form' and on a lighter note: 'This House believes that ghosts are dead.'

The Cinema Club showed films of merit – 'Lord of the Flies', 'Billy Budd', 'Animal Farm' and 'The Loneliness of the Long Distance Runner.'

The Geological Society took trips to Alderley Edge, Castleton, Scarborough, Snowdonia, and visited Ireland to see the Giant's Causeway.

The Junior Christian Fellowship was proud to include among its many speakers an ex-member of staff Martin Boysen, who talked about his experiences on the Mount Everest Expedition. He could not make the final summit because his equipment failed, but a far worse tragedy was the loss of one of the team. *"And yet we were successful. It had been a happy expedition, with excellent teamwork. Not everyone can get to the top in the same way that not everyone can score a winning goal. The personal disappointment of not reaching the top will always be there; the loss of one of my best friends is a permanent hurt. Climbing, like life, has its light and shade."*

An Ornithology Group started up – boys were enthusiastic and enjoyed several outings to various reserves.

The Canal Club took boys to Inverness to cruise the Caledonian Canal.

Members of the Aero-Modelling Club flew their aircraft in Lyme Park, where, despite windy conditions, the craft achieved speeds averaging 75mph.

The Photographic, English and Mountaineering Societies also prospered and grew in membership.

The Debating Society competing at the European Youth Parliament Finals in 2009 at Durham University.

Commonwealth Day was known as 'Empire Day' in 1912. Its focus today is on unity, human rights, education and economic development, and to bind countries together in peace.

1990-2012

ALTRINCHAM GRAMMAR SCHOOL FOR BOYS

ARTS SOCIETY presents

MURDER AT THE MANOR

An audience of very special house guests is invited to join ROY COLEMAN ROBERT FITT and school staff for an intimate evening at mysterious Heatherington Manor.

You will be received in the Main Hall at ALTRINCHAM GRAMMAR SCHOOL FOR BOYS (Heath Road, Hale, entrance) on SATURDAY 24 NOVEMBER at 7.00 for 7.30pm

Black tie optional

ADMISSION (includes a Hot Pot supper)
Arts Society Members £5.00 Non Members £6.00

For the attention of: Mrs Kath Dennis, Altrincham Grammar School for Boys, Marlborough Road, Bowdon, Cheshire WA14 2RS

I enclose £ .... (cheques payable to AGS Arts Society) as payment for .... ticket(s) for Murder at the Manor which should be sent to:

Name ....

Address ....

ARTS SOCIETY presents A 60th anniversary party for VE-DAY!

Daily Mirror

ALTRINCHAM GRAMMAR SCHOOL FOR BOYS

SATURDAY 7TH MAY

1940s DRESS IS WELCOME

FEATURING ...

- songs and sing-along with Ginny Murray and Alison Wormersley
- a selection of readings from the era
- the school swing band with 'Glenn Miller-style' music of the era
- talk on Lord Bowdon by Ginny Murray
- 'jitterbug' and other dance routines from the June Rendell School of Dancing
- a duet from Bob Gledhill and Tim Shorten
- accordianist
- address from Lord Mountbatten's secretary

Programmes from the Arts Society events.

The first expedition of the Fell Walking Group began with a gruelling day on the Glyders in North Wales, and over the years several walks in the Lake District and the Peak District were arranged.

About half of Year 12 took part in Community Service; they helped children with physical and learning difficulties by playing football, teaching them to swim, and reading to them.

The Amnesty Group sent Christmas cards to prisoners of conscience and backed a campaign to stop the export of armoured vehicles, and weapons sent to countries which used them for torture.

Commonwealth Day was observed annually in Westminster Abbey and for several years boys attended the services. Royalty and politicians added interest to the occasion and the event reflected the different cultural traditions of member nations.

The Science Society changed its name to BAYS (British Association of Young Scientists). It visited the University of Manchester and museums, invited speakers into the School, encouraging boys to have fun and enjoy science.

Members of the Electronics Club and the Computer Design Club worked on many different projects. A Year 12 student was awarded the title of Young Engineer for Britain with his GCSE project on a fluid suspension seat post for mountain bikes. The Guitar Building Group encouraged members to *"make the guitar of your dreams."* More than 130 guitars have been made.

The Arts Society was established in 1998 and brought together parents, teachers and boys on its committee. Its aim was to broaden the scope of arts related activities at the School. A memorable event was when the committee invited Jasper Carrott to talk to members. He gave an exclusive lesson in comedy, teaching how to be a comedian, leaving his audience in fits of laughter by a stream of spontaneous gags. The following year Andrew Motion, Poet Laureate came into the School. He said he believed it was within his remit to write about contentious issues, in particular his criticism of western leaders' basis for war. The Arts Society hosted an evening to celebrate the 100th Anniversary of Walt Disney's birth, at which the only person with a PhD in Disney Studies gave a most enjoyable talk and slide show.

The School has a variety of societies of different faiths. The Islamic Association, Hindu Society and Christian Union remain very strong and more recently an inter-faith society called *Co-exist* was formed. It promotes good relations, understanding and respect between people of different faiths. *Through dialogue we will be one step closer to a more peaceful world. We will always be stronger together than we could ever be apart.*

The Music Club and below the Lego Mindstorms Club

During my time abroad as a volunteer I was told: *"Many people come, bring things, and go again. You come with your heart. I was shot at and shelled, but it is better to light one candle than to curse the darkness."*

"Returning to my Primary School, I helped children with spelling, reading, simple maths and computer work. When I volunteered as Father Christmas the children saw through my disguise – I was wearing my own shoes!"

Charities

Staff and students at AGSB have an impressive record of generosity in raising funds and awareness of good causes. There are many unsung heroes who take part in events from bag packing in local stores to organising a whole year group in a fund-raising event. Recently there has been a focus around boys who were pupils at AGSB, but died during their years here. "Chad's Challenges" was formed to remember Chad Mulholland who lost his three year battle with Hodgkin's Lymphoma, and the money raised goes principally to the Young Oncology Unit at the Christie Hospital. "*Chad wanted to help others and was so positive and upbeat despite everything he was going through; he was a real fighter.*" In 2011 Chad's Challenges was awarded the "Diana Certificate of Excellence." Rob Anderson was another student who lost his life during his time at AGSB when he suffered from a severe asthma attack on his way home from football. His many friends led a campaign to raise awareness of asthma and the school held an afternoon of sports to raise funds, because sports was Robert's passion. This is another example of the kindness, resourcefulness and determination of AGSB boys.

During the first half of the 2009 term, pupils raised over £3,400 in a series of activities. The School donated £2,400 to the Children's Adventure Farm, £500 to EducAid for schools in Sierra Leone, and £500 to a world wide charity which supplies books to schools. It also supported Barnardo's, Children in Need, Jeans for Genes, Lepra, Teenage Cancer Trust and the Willow Foundation to name but a few. Community Service volunteers helped in the local community in a wide variety of ways. One Year 12 wrote: "*My volunteer work sent me to a care home where I spent time interacting with the elderly residents. I enjoyed talking to individuals who have full and interesting lives and can more fully appreciate this often undervalued but hugely important group. What people want is your time and I hope it has made me a more considerate person.*"

Boys have also worked abroad in Slovenia and Calcutta; here they helped in refugee camps, played football and Bingo, talked to the inmates and listened to their concerns. "*They cannot work or plan for the future – they wait and pray.*" AGSB boys did what they could for AIDS victims and drug addicts; volunteers have built roads, drains and shelters. Boys will try anything!

Volunteer runners for the Chad's Challenges Marathon 2009

Rob Anderson Day 2010

For the past four years, the PFA (the Parents' and Friends Association) has raised over £20,000 a year for the School. The money has been used for sports equipment, to kit out the Food Technology room and to purchase interactive white boards for use across the School.

The P.F.A

The Parents' and Friends Association raises money for the School and at the same time offers an opportunity for parents, teachers and friends of the School to enjoy some great occasions. It has been incredibly successful in raising thousands of pounds each year. Over the years the committee has organised a variety of events; new ideas have included car boot sales, a fashion show, and entertainment by the staff group 'Band-Age.' In 1992, a joint event with the Girls School was the Duck Race. 1,250 ducks were launched on a stretch of the River Bollin and retrieved further downstream. Identifying the winner proved somewhat controversial!

The first major gift to the School was a minibus, which was used constantly by the sports teams, chess clubs, community service and for field work. In the same year the Parents' and Friends Association donated the Nimbus Computer system, having raised the necessary funds. More recently, a highlight of each year has been the Swing Band Night when parents are entertained by the nationally recognised School Swing Band.

AGSB had been extremely fortunate in having such an enterprising and enthusiastic Parents' and Friends Association, which does so much vital work for the School.

The Old Altrinchamians

The Old Boys Association is still active and flourishing. The Old Boys meet several times a year for reunions and an annual Dinner. The Saville Laver Memorial Dinner, inaugurated in 1998 is held at an Oxbridge College and attended by Old Boys and staff (past and present). The Annual Dinner is held locally with a guest speaker and a great deal of conviviality and happy reminiscing. Stories which bear repeating include memories of Mr Bickers such as his apocryphal remark; on learning that the Inspectors were due to visit the school replied "Will that be gas, electricity or sanitary?" His standard response to reduce his ever-mounting in-tray of paper was BTBT ("bin the b...... thing").

The Old Boys have football teams which play in local leagues with considerable success and a Golf Section which organises tournaments against staff and boys and which competes in regional competitions against other Old Boys Societies. Each year the Old Boys make a generous donation to the School for the support of extra curricular activities.

The Swing Band playing with German Exchange students 2008

Old Altrinchamians at the Annual Dinner 2011

Baden-Powell tested his ideas for 'Scouting for Boys' on younger boys during camp on Brownsea Island, and this book became the 4th best seller of the twentieth century.

Baden-Powell (1857–1941) shared the same birthday February 22nd, as his wife, Olive. It became known as 'Founder's Day' by the Scouts, and 'Thinking Day' by the Guides.

1962-2012

1961 Members of the Group took part in the gruelling Four Inns Walk for the first time – a one-day race across 50 miles of hills and high moors of Derbyshire, from Holme Bridge to Buxton taking in Black Hill, Bleaklow and Kinder Scout. It is a tradition that has been continued over the years.

1963 On 6th July the Group celebrated its Golden Jubilee with a camp and displays on the School field. The event was attended by past and present members, parents and friends in the presence of Lord Stamford and many Scouting and Civic dignitaries.

1966 The 'new look' for Scouts was introduced.

- Shorts and the iconic 'scout hat' were replaced by long trousers and a beret.
- Senior Scouts and Rover Scouts were disbanded to be replaced by Venture Scouts.

1967-1973 Scouting was branching out into more adventurous activities. Although training camps still taught traditional skills, mountain skills courses in the Lake District were introduced along with hostelling and hiking expeditions at half-terms. These trips have continued to this day and now also embrace mountain biking.

1975 14th May will always be remembered as the day of the fire, when the Scout Headquarters building was badly damaged by a fire. Although many contents, including archives, were lost much was saved. Repairs took two years to complete.

1979 A new Venture Scout section was started after many years without one.

1983 In an attempt to extend the repertoire of adventurous activities members of the Group ran the Manchester Marathon, climbed the British Three Peaks (Snowdon, Scafell Pike and Ben Nevis) in under 24 hours, and undertook their first international expedition to Norway.

1988 To mark the Group's 75th birthday, members undertook the first of many expeditions to the International Scout Centre in Kandersteg, Switzerland. These trips enabled Scouts to take part in much more adventurous activities than they could in the UK including climbing to over 6,000m to stay in some of the high mountain huts, and hiking across glaciers. Other activities included mountain biking, crate stacking and rock climbing, but the main benefit was to meet Scouts from other countries around the world.

Jamborees – Over the years members of the Group have been fortunate enough to have been selected to represent their district and country at World Scout Jamborees. These events are only held every four years and bring together over 40,000 young people from around the world in one massive camp. Members have been to camps in Australia, Korea, Holland and Sweden. In 2007, the Jamboree was held in the UK to celebrate the Centenary of the Scouting Movement. Two members of 3rd Altrincham Scouts attended but many more visited for the day.

*

In his final letter to the Scouts before he retired, Baden-Powell wrote: *"I believe God put us in this world to be happy and enjoy life, remember that happiness does not come from being rich or self-indulgent. Try to leave this world a little better than you found it."*

3rd Altrincham Scout Troop

The School donated £50 to the new Royal Exchange Theatre to have a commemorative seat. It is A17, between seats donated by Christopher Plummer and Richard Attenborough.

The Spring Concert involved many soloists, and featured 'Sir Freddie Crisp and the Elephants'. Unbelievably this turned out to be weatherman Fred Talbot and a rock band!

School productions: 1962 onwards

'Caesar and Cleopatra' was the production in 1962; *Caesar was an efficient and relaxed Emperor – a fine piece of acting. The architecture of ancient Egypt was convincing, an ancient steam engine and music played on a variety of glasses added authenticity*. This was followed by 'A Man for all Seasons.' The next production 'Escape', which ran in London in 1926 and is one of Galsworthy's most successful plays. It is about people's reactions to an escaped convict and the actors had to perform many different characters, doing so most convincingly.

'Billy Budd' proved to be an excellent production of Herman Melville's novel, with splendid acting and smooth team work. The audience were judges between their conscience and the law, in a play which presented the stark values of life and death. Two plays were produced in one year – 'Toad of Toad Hall' and 'Romanoff and Juliet.'

Oliver was a zestful production that never flagged, starting with 'Food, Glorious Food.' This time it was good to know that the female parts were played by girls!

'The Tempest' proved a great challenge to the director, but we easily accepted the actors completely as characters in the play. The performances were good all round – a dignified Prospero, convincing eloquence, and a very regal King Alonso.

'Pirates of Penzance' was chosen as a gesture to Mr Crowther to mark his impending retirement, reminding him of his early days at the School. 'Cox and Box' and 'Death of a Salesman' were contrasting productions; the latter conveyed the love and anger of Willy so that we felt the sadness and waste inherent in his death at the end. These were followed by 'The Merchant of Venice' and 'David and Goliath.' The next productions were 'Twelfth Night' and 'All the King's Men'. 'The Pied Piper' was a short musical, for which two members of staff wrote the script and the music. 'Peer Gynt' was an enigmatic play about the search for identity and the power of love, starting with the blind impetuousness of youth, through experiences of maturity to the achieved wisdom of old age. 'The Royal Hunt of the Sun' was a play rich in ideas – personal, political and religious, offering thoughtful entertainment while all the time a dazzling sun dominated the action. This was followed at the end of the year by 'A Christmas Carol.'

The orchestra rehearsed regularly, performing at the Christmas Concert and morning service. It was most encouraging to see the interest in instrumental playing among the junior boys, and the comment "*A school should be proud to contain and support such talent. I hope that ours is*" proved very appropriate.

The 'Mayall Voices' catered for the senior boys, winning many prestigious awards at competitions run by The National Festival for Youth. The present Barbershop Choir flourishes, singing at both local and School events.

Drama & Music

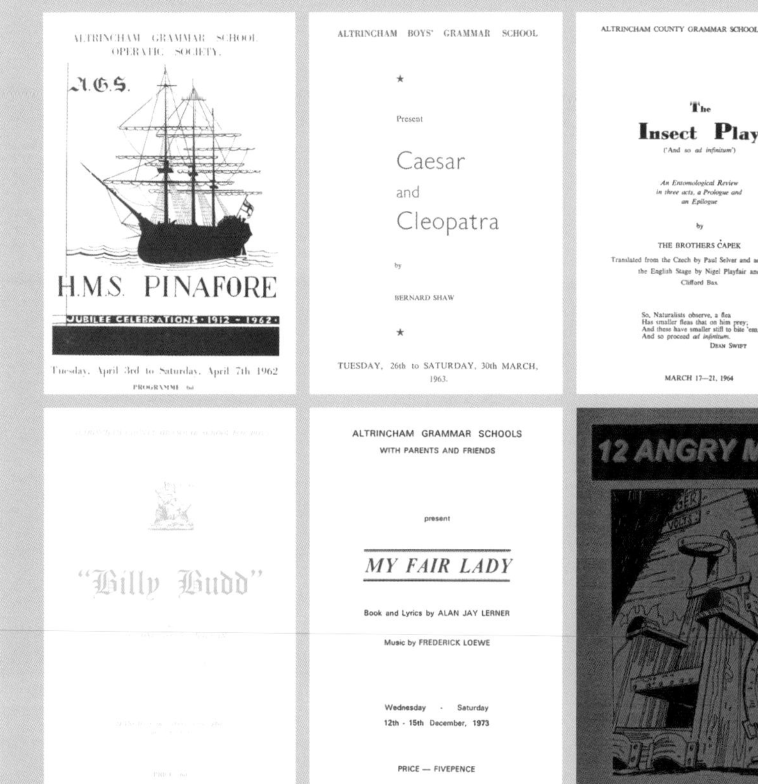

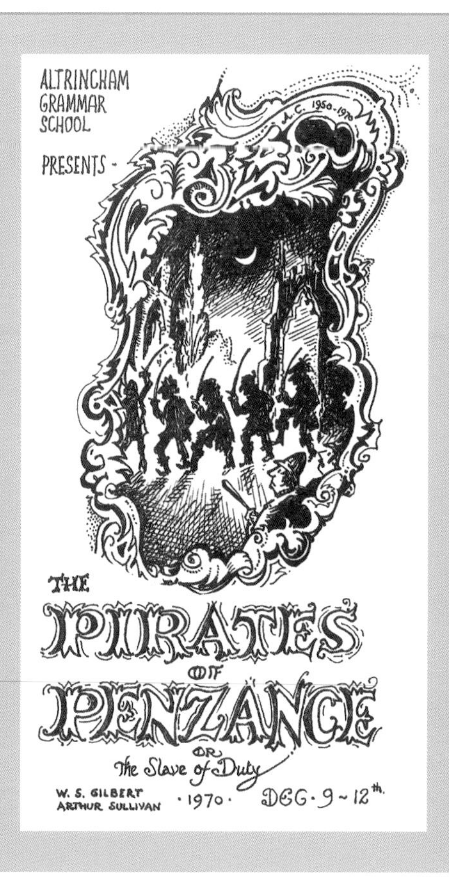

'Journey's End' was a play designed to make the audience face the waste and futility of war. The poignancy of the play was conveyed by the contrast between the gloom of the dug-out and the fragile flicker of the candles (which were extinguished in the final scene). The following year 'Androcles and the Lion' provided a mixture of romance and comedy. The staff room was eloquently portrayed in 'No More Sitting on the Old School Bench' with its chaos of books, tatty furniture and broken down equipment.

'Gallows Glorious' was the School play in 1984 marking the 50th anniversary of its first performance. The play focuses on the character of John Brown and the drama raises interesting questions about his belief in a cause.

'Hands Across the Sea' by Noel Coward was a complete contrast. It parodied the decaying world of the disintegrating Empire – when characters sip endless cocktails *"it's absolutely divine darling, terribly divine"*. 'Don't Drink the Water' by Woody Allen was an affectionate send up of his fellow Americans and the disastrous consequences of a young ambassador who believed in the honest truth as opposed to the diplomatic truth. 'Beyond Reasonable Doubt' left the audience in a state of uncertainty as to whodunnit. The second half suggested that the evidence heard previously might not have been the whole truth and surely no man would murder such a wife who portrayed domestic bliss so convincingly? In the same year 'All the King's Men' told the true story behind 'Humpty Dumpty.' 'A Man for all Seasons', about Thomas More, written by Robert Bolt, was followed by 'Sherlock Holmes' but with a different ending, not at the Reichenbach Falls this time. Then followed a farce 'Cat Among the Pigeons.' The plot centred on two households and two sisters; sexual pursuits were acted out with bewildering speed, rapid exits, and trousers falling down revealing a puce coloured pair of long combinations with hearts attached!

A large guillotine, a severed head and the sound of knitting needles set the atmosphere and gave authenticity to 'The Scarlet Pimpernel', the 1996 production. Orczy's play is a grim reminder of the fall of the French aristocracy; only the elusive Scarlet Pimpernel – that guardian of justice – can save them. His identity provides the mystery; it can't possibly be the foppish Sir Percy Blakeney, can it?

The production in 2011, 'Return to the Forbidden Planet' was a superb mixture of drama and music. The musical numbers took shape with our own band and singers, boys were choreographed with stunning success (including skating) and the make-up department did the boys proud.

Recent Productions:

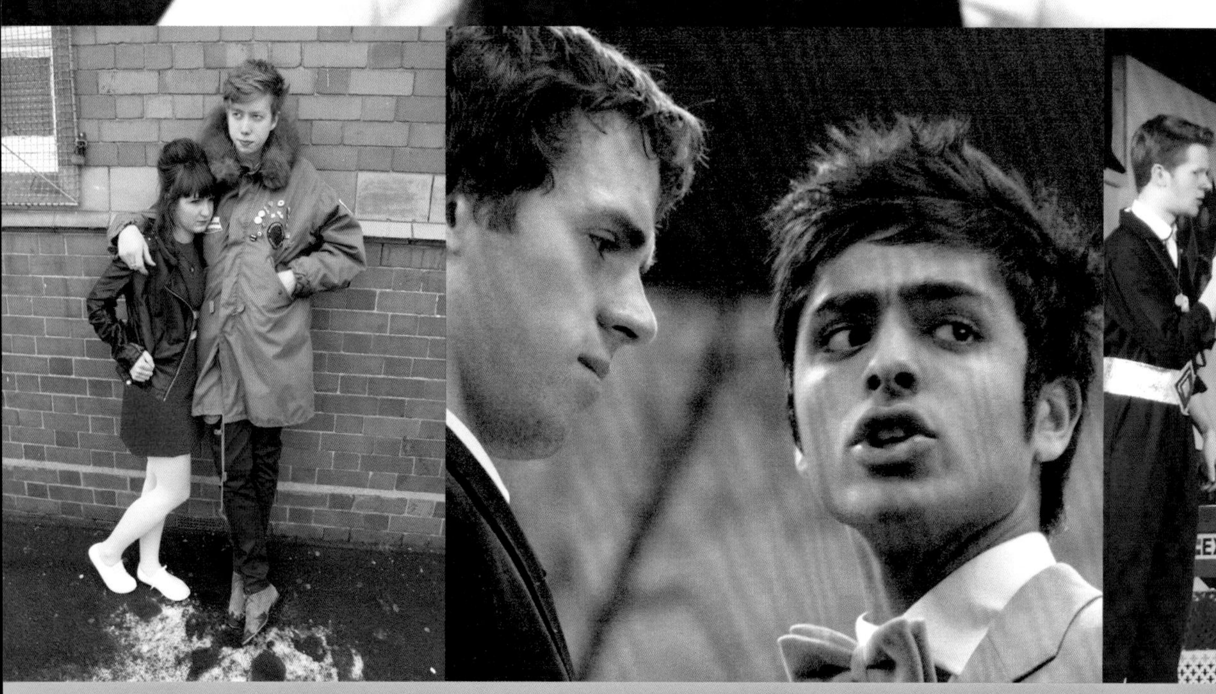

Romeo and Juliet 2010

The Importance of being Earnest 2008

Return to the Forbidden Planet 2011

Drama & Music

A Midsummer Nights Dream 2008

The History Boys 2009

Romeo and Juliet 2010

England won the 1966 FIFA World Cup after defeating Germany 4-2. Before the tournament the Jules Rimet trophy was stolen. It was discovered wrapped in newspaper by a dog called Pickles under a bush in London.

The 1962 World Cup, held in Chile, was won by Brazil. In 1970 the World Cup was held in Mexico (the first to be hosted in N. America). Pele was playing his fourth and final World Cup and Brazil beat Italy 4-1.

The name 'Ashes' was born after England lost a match in 1882. A spoof obituary was published stating English cricket had died, the body will be cremated and the ashes taken to Australia. The next tour was dubbed *"The quest to regain the Ashes."*

1962 - 80

In 1962 the three senior football teams played a total of 55 games through the season and altogether the School played 149 fixtures. The hockey team provided players for the county, there were badminton and basketball teams and two boys were chosen to play basketball for the county.

Stuart Roberts was selected as a member of the British Olympics Swimming Team in the 1968 Mexico Olympics.

There were so many sporting opportunities in the School that in 1960 AGSB became the yardstick by which all other Cheshire schools were judged for the allocation of sports funding.

Mexico Olympics: J. S. Roberts took part in the Olympic Games as a member of the England Swimming team.

Cross Country Team 1964

Why Britain needs tiddlywinks

An increasingly large number of prejudiced people choose to make the game of Tiddlywinks the object of mockery. The severest critics are always those who have chosen not to play the game. "There is no skill in Tiddlywinks" cry those who have never seen a player meticulously addressing a wink with a quidger, judging the exact angle, distance, and pressure needed for an intricate squop shot. Tiddlywinks calls for the coordination of mind and body, a dexterity and finesse far greater than the layman imagines. It demands delicacy, accuracy, controlled power, concentration and tactics. It represents a power for good throughout the country.

AGSB enters Guinness Book of Records

In 1964 two players were selected to play for England in the Annual International Tiddlywinks Championship against Scotland. AGSB was the first school to provide a pair for the England team and they won all their games. The 1964 National Championship was dominated by AGSB players. Out of the last eight pairs left in the knockout competition, seven were from the School. AGSB entered the Guinness Book of Records.

In 1968 sailing was established in the School. Cheshire Schools' Sailing and Canoeing Association had existed for many years but canoeing was more popular. Once Tatton Mere was opened for sailing it was decided the School should take advantage of it. The first dinghy was a Heron, built by boys and staff using the designer's drawings. "*One difficulty in the construction was that no two lines are parallel and no two pieces of wood square to each other, but our techniques were transformed into those of the boat builder.*" After 14 months of work, Heron 6286 *Barbara* was launched, followed by an Enterprise *Gillian*.

High Jump

Judo Club 1967

South African Zola Budd twice broke the women's 500m world record. She was unusual as she trained and raced barefoot. She applied for British citizenship to avoid the sporting boycott of South Africa winning a place on the British Olympic team in 1984.

Linford Christie, former sprinter, is the only British man to win gold in the 100m at all four major competitions open to British athletes. He was also the first European to break the 10 second barrier in the 100m. He is Britain's most decorated male athlete.

1980-90

"A sports survey revealed that 53% of boys played sport for the School and over 80% of those boys said they enjoyed doing so."

In weight lifting, or the Art of Pondertollation, *"we were introduced to the basic principles of addressing the bar and a multitude of styles of lifts: clean, jerk, bench-press, bicep-curl, all with 50lb, 80lb and 115lb bars.*

The School offered a wide range of sporting activities – soccer, rugby, cross country, swimming, badminton, cricket, athletics, volley ball, soft ball and weight training. Cricket gained in popularity when the new pavilion, funded by the Parents' and Friends Association, was opened.

Four Sixth Formers qualified as Instructors with the Royal Yachting Association – becoming 'advanced sailors.' Four boys represented AGSB in the National Schools Sailing Regatta; one returned with a trophy and the School swept the board in all classes.

A cycle tour of 3,000 miles went to France, Italy, Switzerland, Germany, Luxemburg, and Belgium. Six boys were selected to swim in the County Championships, and one boy represented Cheshire.

Judo became extremely popular. Boys represented the county at soccer, cricket, cycling, swimming, badminton, and chess. Two boys represented England at an International Tiddlywinks Conference. Three golfers played in the English School's National Golf Championships. AGSB won Junior under 15 and under 16 Single Sculls in the Northwest Junior Rowing Championships and won two Silver medals in the Sailing Regatta. The under 15's won the Trafford Schools' Tennis League for four years in succession. The School represented Greater Manchester in English Schoolboys Soccer, and came fifth in the National Cycling Competition.

Paul Allott

In 1986 Mark Redman was selected to swim for English schools and Paul Thomas was the Cheshire Open Golf Champion.

However it was in cricket that the School hit the headlines most frequently in the late 1970s and 1980s because AGSB was where Paul Allott had played his School cricket.

Paul Allott

On Tuesday August 11th 1982 Paul was picked to represent his country in his first Test Match in Australia. Only three months before at the start of a new season, all he was concerned about was securing a place in Lancashire's First Team; now he was to play against Australia – the one country that every cricketer would die to play against, to beat and secure the ashes for good old England! Only a few weeks before, England had come back from the brink of an innings defeat to beat Australia and level the series. Paul wrote *"If I were to trace back my career and ambitions it is true to say it all started at AGSB. It was one of those lucky things that my year was a particularly talented one, but for me, it was cricket that held all the charm, mystery and challenge. When we won the Cheshire Knockout Cup it was then that I realised cricket was for me, not just as a recreation or a pastime but a way of earning a living. My most exhilarating moment in my career was when I took my first test match wicket. If there is ever a better moment for me I hope I am there when it happens!"*

Paul now is a commentator on Sky Sports.

In 1993 the Staff football team toured Oxford, causing a stir out of proportion to its degree of success. Unnatural selection meant that fossil specimens had a combined age of 4004. They won 7 of 15 games, and are far from extinct!

Brothers, Ian and Mark Roberts, have both held Regional and National Junior Championship Windsurfing titles. In 1997 they were part of the British team for the Junior World Windsurfing Championships in Spain.

Staff can play football too!

"Staff football's chief contribution this year has not been to our national games, rather to our national health service so numerous and serious were our injuries. So many different players were tried out that at times it was hard to work out whether we were attacking or defending, especially as most of those involved do not concern themselves unduly with which direction they hoof the ball. But speed isn't everything, neither is skill. JB incorporated orienteering into his midfield role, rushing pointlessly from point to point. JW contributed a good fracture, and the fatalities mounted."

"Anyone who had a pair of boots was picked. Fortunately we were blessed with a series of injuries which allowed us to co-opt Sixth Formers who still possessed a functioning cardio-vascular system. PN tirelessly atoned for the miscalculations of his less sprightly colleagues. The versatility of MK knew no bounds and his anguished tackles and apologies to referees were worthy of a place in Barcelona's first team. AB displayed immaculate tackling, at times using only one leg. The capable WS was helped by his myopia; JB and JH relied on bad knees, varicose veins and related cognitive weaknesses for their excuses. All goals were greeted with delighted astonishment. KP was always on hand to lash the ball in which ever direction he happened to be facing. PD paraded his skills in midfield whenever he could get back that far. GH played with a great deal of height, and KK with a great deal of pain"

AGSB Football

Girls versus Boys

In 1991 after seven days of continuous rain, the scene was set for the 'Golden Welly' Girls versus Lads Rugby Match to raise money for Comic Relief. Both teams were impeded by the mud but one girl *"achieved her own brand of magic by playing 59 minutes of Rugby in the worst conditions experienced this century yet kept her white T-shirt absolutely spotless."* Cheered on by an ecstatic entourage of fans, wading through the quagmire, the boys scored the winning try.

AGSB First XV Students versus Old Boys XV

2005: *"I was chosen to play Rugby for Cheshire and became Captain, then selected for the North of England under 16 team. I was tried out for an England team, England A, and played against Wales, France and Canada. I am honoured to have been selected to play rugby for England"* Chris Davis

50 years of PE and Games to celebrate.
In the 1960s and 70s whilst PE and some extra-curricular games were taught and organised by the two members of the PE department, many sports were led and organised by some exceptional teachers whose commitment to extra-curricular sport was exemplary. One such was Roy Wilson who was described as:
"Yorkshire's gift to Altrincham Grammar. When it came to infusing boys with enthusiasm for cricket he had no equal and if anything, he gave even more commitment to football."

Paul Allott benefited from Roy Wilson's cricket coaching before going on to play professionally for Lancashire and then representing England.

Gradually, by the mid 1970s the PE department assumed greater responsibility for all School sport, but was still enormously reliant on non-specialist staff to assist in running teams.
Even today that remains the case although the department has increased in size considerably. Roger Cleland gave 30 years to teaching countless boys to sail to the highest standard; 'Nick' Nicholls devoted hours to coaching squash before moving on to canoeing and Peter Butler ran the 1st XI for more than 30 years.

We have enjoyed the high levels of sporting success gained by many AGSB boys and, whilst not possible to mention them all here, a few examples would include:

Rugby:
Richard and David Wilks, Rob Worsfold, Chris Davies – County and National Schoolboy Level.

Football:
Paul McGuiness, Matthew Jones, Andrew Smart, Vernon Rowland – Professional Football.

Hockey: Richie Dawson-Smith – possible Olympics 2012.

J. Hughes

AGSB win the rugby Andy Hindle Cup 2011

First European football tour 2011

George Li is now ranked first in England under 17 Doubles; fifth in England under 17 Singles and has reached the under 17 England Badminton squad. His ambition is now to push for Commonwealth and Olympic squads.

In 2008 the first ever South Trafford Table Tennis Competition was held in *The Grammar*. Each of Year 7, 8 and 9 had three players who played superb table tennis and the overall winners became South Trafford Champions.

2000-12

2000 The rugby team was described as having "*dynamic tactics, and hugely talented defenders.*"

2001 The School entered the Trafford Basketball League for the first time and the team played some stunning games. Boys playing football "*threw themselves into the sport, trying to earn their place with a never-give-up attitude.*" Three boys were on the books of professional clubs.

2002 Year 7 Cross Country team won the Cheadle Hulme School event and two represented Manchester in the Greater Manchester Schools Championships.

2003 For the first time AGSB won the Cheshire Schools Dewes Cup for cricket, held at Chester, winning all seven games.

The under 15 Rugby team progressed to the third round of the Daily Mail Cup. Players were described as "*strong, powerful, alert and tenacious*" and two boys made it into the Cheshire Squad.

In the British Schools Tennis Championships the under 16's doubles pair won the title.

In Football the under 14's were a talented squad, "*scoring many goals with first class performances*".

2004 AGSB won the under 18 North Cheshire Schools Tennis Championships and two of the team became the North of England Champions.

Four boys were under 16 North West Badminton Champions, and the basketball team became Trafford under 14 Champions.

2005 Chris Davies played rugby for England; Chris Kumeta played baseball for Great Britain.

The under 15 football had the most successful season in its career.

The under 16 basketball team won 5 out of their 6 games; the under 14's were the Trafford Champions.

2006 This was a hugely successful year for the hockey teams with both under 14 and under 16 teams becoming the North West champions.

The under 14 basketball team reached the semi-finals of the Schools League.

In the Trafford Schools' Cross Country, AGSB won the Year 8 and 9 age group team and took third place overall.

2007 The under 15's went on their first rugby tour to the Isle of Man.

"*The main reasons for our improvement are hard work and muddy practices.*"

There were so many enthusiastic Year 9 boys who turned up to play basketball, that two teams were started up.

2008 *The Grammar* was opened; *all major sports can be catered for - hockey, tennis, rugby, football and cricket and the indoor multi use hall can accommodate basketball, trampolining, table tennis, dance, martial arts and gymnastics.*

2009 Year 7 rugby won the Cheshire State Schools Cup. The Year 9 rugby team went to Holland and won all their games. Two Year 8 boys were selected to play rugby for the Lancashire County squad.

A Year 12 student has been selected to join a lacrosse team to travel to the USA and is now regarded as one of the best under 19 lacrosse players in England.

Year 10 footballers entered the Trafford Cup Competition, and against all the Trafford teams they reached the semi-finals.

Year 7 Rugby reached the semi-finals of the Sevens Tournament.

2010 The first South Trafford Table Tennis Competition was held at *The Grammar* for Years 7, 8 and 9. AGSB were the overall winners. The table tennis team "*was crowned the 4th best school in the country, a great achievement on our first attempt in the competition. All the boys performed brilliantly.*"

2011 The first European Football tour of Spain took place. The under 14 team won all their matches and the boys' high level skills were commended.

The AGSB tennis team won under 12's, under 14's and under 16's in the same year. It is the only school ever to have held these three titles at the same time.

Sports & Games

*

In 2010 the fifth annual British Schools Karting Championships was won by a trio of students from AGSB, John Gwyneth, Louis Nicholson and Chris Bryant. They fended off competition from over 30 schools.

National Karting Champions 2011 visiting Red Bull racing Headquarters.

50 years of Languages to celebrate
During the last 50 years, language teaching has been completely transformed from the Latin and Greek classes fifty years ago, when boys worked silently on translation and grammar exercises based on literary texts. The thriving Language College and Modern Foreign Languages (MFL) department now teach an impressive range of languages including French, German, Spanish, Arabic, Chinese, Italian, Russian and Japanese. Lessons focus not only on writing, reading and translation, as in the past, but on listening, speaking and cultural aspects.

MFL classrooms are lively and noisy and activities have interactive computer based learning as well as group and pair work. Cross-curricular activities take place linking languages with other subjects and we also teach languages in our partner primary schools.

Since gaining Language College status in 2003, the MFL department has seen many exciting developments: we have introduced new languages within and outside the curriculum, for students, staff and the wider community. We offer boys additional qualifications such as Asset Languages, CBLC French, German and Spanish for Business and the ASDAN International award. Our classrooms are equipped with interactive whiteboards and we have two multi-media digitised language labs where boys practice speaking and listening, learning the language at their own pace.

MFL exchanges take place annually with partner schools in France, Germany and Spain, boys experiencing different cultures at first hand and practicing their language skills. Language College Immersion Courses to China, Russia and the Middle East have taken intrepid boys and staff to far flung destinations, as

Trips & Excursions

Language College Exchanges

have our links with the Apeejay schools in Delhi. In our Centenary year we will develop further links with the Beijing 101 School in China.

Underpinning the changes over the past 50 years is the recognition that our boys are global citizens, they have the opportunity to live and work all over the world and will gain intercultural understanding as well as valuable communication and language skills during their time at AGSB.

H. Meadowcroft

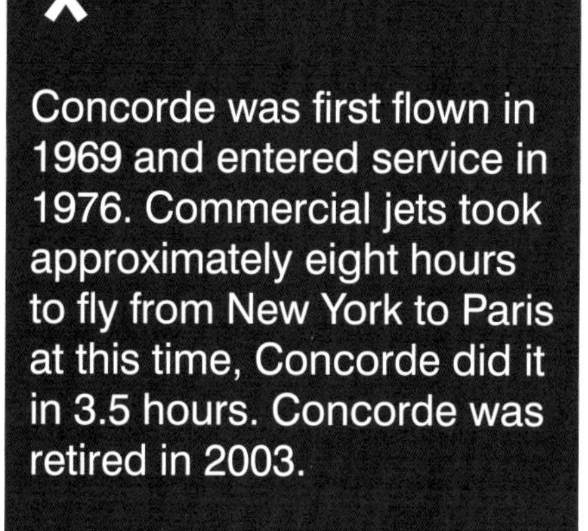

*

Concorde was first flown in 1969 and entered service in 1976. Commercial jets took approximately eight hours to fly from New York to Paris at this time, Concorde did it in 3.5 hours. Concorde was retired in 2003.

Trips & Excursions

1962 onwards

The majority of trips between 1960 and 1990 were to destinations in the British Isles, many organised by departments with an educational agenda. But there was no shortage of places to visit or boys wanting to be included. There were Geology and Geography visits to appropriate sites, History visits to York, Chester, and Hadrian's Wall, English trips to Brontë country and Stratford, plus many theatre visits and Science trips to museums, universities, exhibitions and later to Futuroscope. The fun excursions for the Ramblers were to Arran and the Lake District – anywhere there were tracks to follow, and the Railway Society went all over the country.

From 1962 to 1968 the only destination abroad was France, usually Normandy, but one successful week was spent in Souillac, 100 miles east of Bordeaux. The town had been unchanged for centuries, clustered around a disused monastery. From there boys visited the prehistoric caverns at Lascaux.

In 1968, the skiing trip was to Resia, Austria and was a great success; breathtaking views and glaring white snow. Boys had two hours practice, two hours instruction, then two hours practice each day and none of them would forget the exhilarating feeling of finally being able to ski downhill. Subsequently there were ski trips and weeks in France (to improve French speaking!) most years.

Gradually more trips abroad were organised. In 1984 the first trip to Germany was arranged – again a great success. Then followed trips to the World War Battlefields in northern France, Poros and Athens in Greece and Rome in Italy. With cheaper air travel in the 1990s horizons soon widened even further.

Trips, excursions and exchange visits went worldwide, and more unusual and varied destinations opened up to students. Every year the School has run trips to France, Germany and Spain to help boys with language. The Geology field trip in Year 13 goes to Cyprus every December - the weather is balmy and the flight and accommodation very good value.

The language trips to Paris, the Rhineland and Barcelona have become legendary as have the ski trips. At first ski trips kept to the Alps and occasionally the Pyrenees but more recently in search of reliable snow and a competitive price locations have become more adventurous - to eastern Europe and across the Atlantic to USA and Canada. The 2008 trip even included a day sight-seeing in New York.

A recent highlight for many a Sixth Former has been the July visit to Venice. First organised by Mr Killian in 2005, since his retirement it has been led by Mrs Barratt and Mrs Harvey-Voyce. The visit combines experiences of high culture with cafe culture. It introduces students to the art of the Renaissance and the cosmopolitan atmosphere of modern Venice.

At the younger end of the School the Year 7 outward bound days in the autumn term have also become a fixture. A variety of locations for the visit have been used but the aim always remains the same. Through activities such as rock climbing,canoeing, abseiling and orienteering the Year 7s learn to work as a team. They also make new friends and often see their teachers in a different light too.

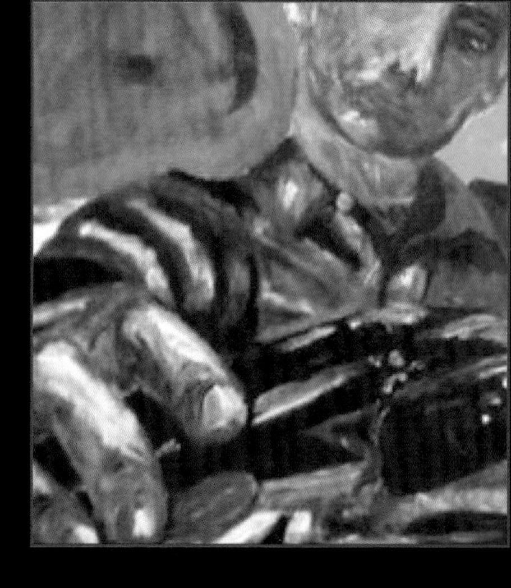

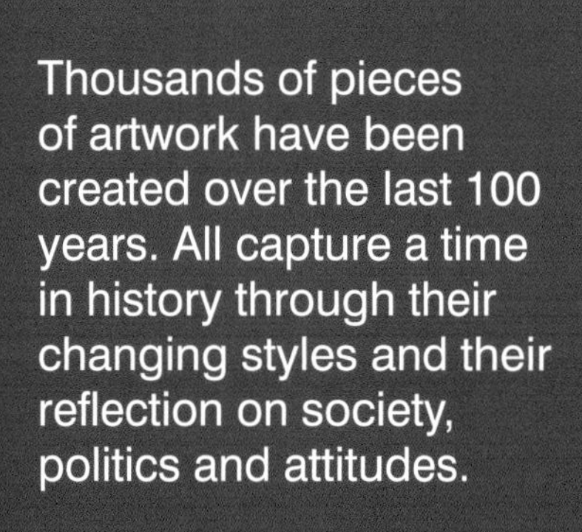

*

Thousands of pieces of artwork have been created over the last 100 years. All capture a time in history through their changing styles and their reflection on society, politics and attitudes.

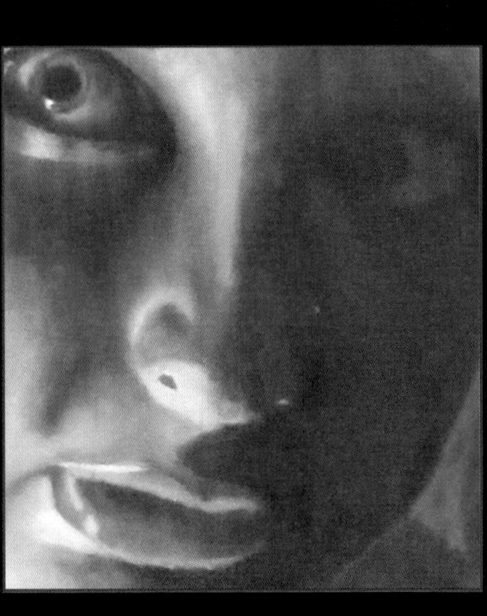

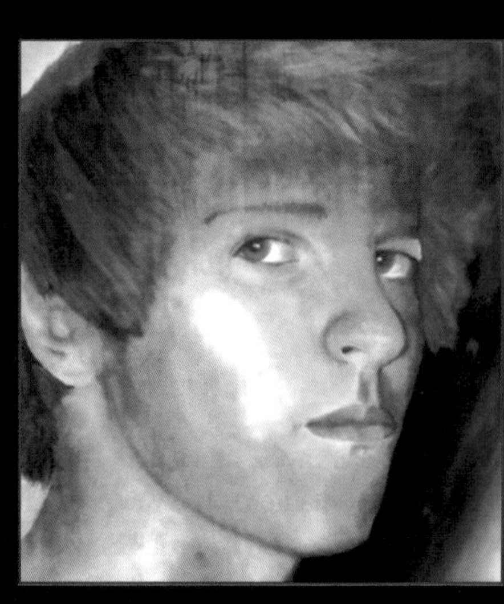

The Turner prize for Art is presented annually to a British artist under the age of 50. It was set up in 1984 to celebrate contemporary art, and consequently is always a controversial event.

1962-2012

The position of Head of any department at AGSB is a coveted role, and there can be no clearer example of that fact than in the Art department. When I became Head of Art in September 1980 I succeeded Bill Mills, who had held the post since the 1940s. Thus there have been only two Heads of Art since the Second World War! Clearly we have both cherished the job.

The black and white photograph below shows Mr Mills teaching his class in the original art room, which still exists as room T4. By the time I arrived here as a rookie 31 years ago however, that room was being used for O Level engineering drawing, and the art room – there was still only one – was the room which Dr Stephen now occupies in the Science Block. For 22 years, I worked somewhat incongruously among the School's scientific community, and I forged some wonderful working friendships with members of the Chemistry staff as a result.

Those twenty-plus years saw several schemes and plans for new art rooms come and go, each one never getting beyond the drawing board stage. When Mrs Hochland joined the staff as the second Art teacher in 1993 we began to use a demountable room by the Scout Hut as a second Art room, until its roof collapsed one severe winter. We then commandeered a cloakroom and knocked through into the boys' toilets to create Art Room 2. Then, apropos of nothing, in 2001 David Wheeldon, the then Head Master, informed me that I was going to get a new room. Yes… I'd heard that one before. Less than a year later however, I was teaching in it.

Now of course, the old cloakroom-toilet conversion has been demolished and replaced by the magnificent new room shown on the right, together with a greatly improved Sixth Form studio. Hence our department is well-accommodated for the next two Heads of Art, who I calculate between them should see the department through to around 2090!

T. Shorten

Art Room 2011

Art Room 1947

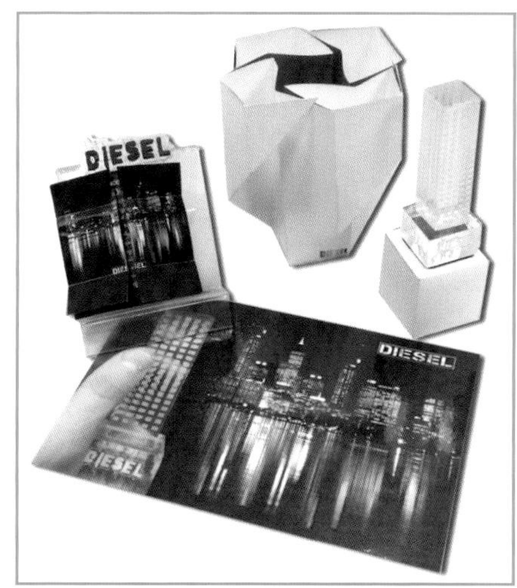

*

"Design is not just what it looks like and feels like. Design is how it works."
Steve Jobs, founder of Apple and Pixar, 1955-2011.

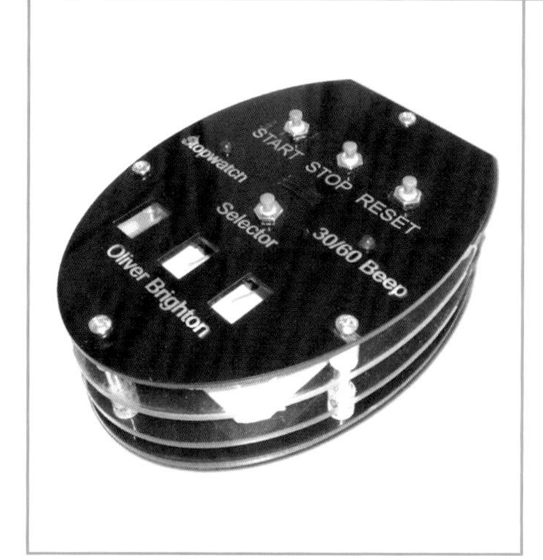

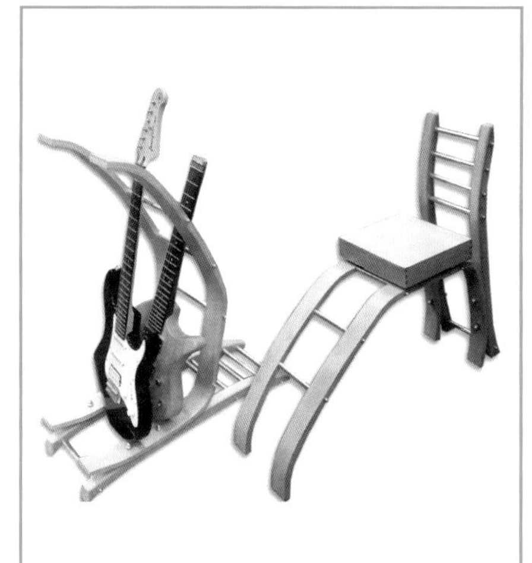

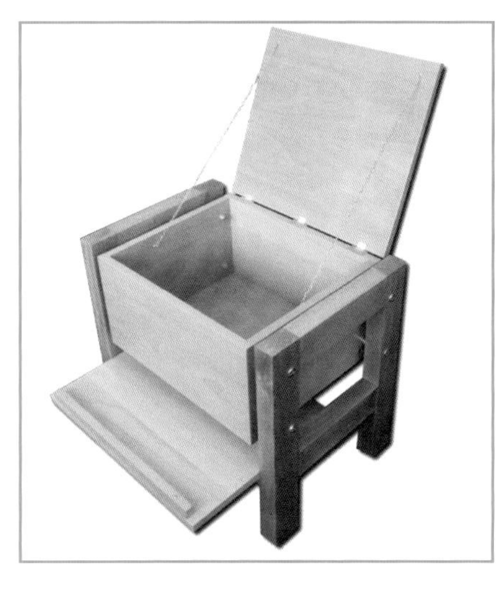

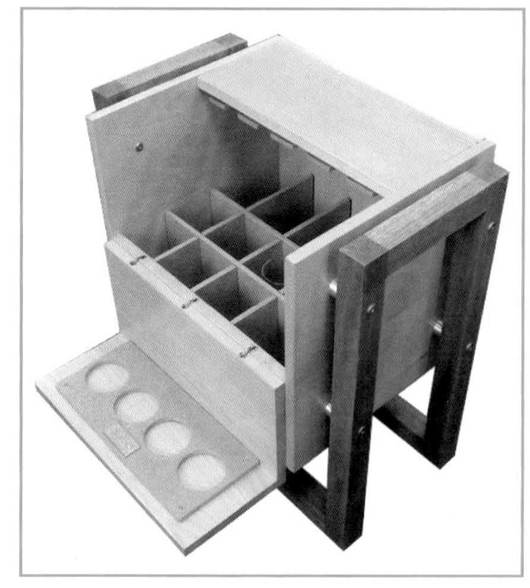

The Design and Technology department started in 1973 and the original small wood lathe, the Startrite Band-saw and the thickness planer still exist and are in Mr Binns' room.

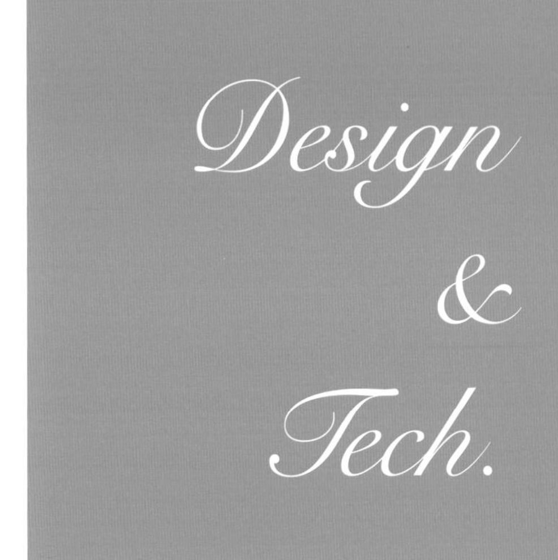

Design & Technology

50 years of success in Design Technology

In 1973 there were three workshops and a drawing office at AGSB; woodwork, metalwork and technical drawing were taught throughout the School. T1 was a woodwork shop, T2 was the metal workshop, T5 was another woodwork shop and upstairs in T4 was the drawing office where engineering drawing was taught. In T2 were three double sided benches with engineer's vices, two pillar drills, pedestal grinder, four centre lathes along the wall, with a milling machine and a linear shaping machine. T5 housed more lathes, a pillar drill, and grinders; and in the drawing office were 25 flip-over drawing desks.

For 25 years a team of four worked together producing interesting projects (including steam engines and wheeled vehicles) and good exam results. The end of the 20th Century brought massive changes to the syllabus and the Technology department morphed into the Design and Technology department. Teachers have come and gone, bringing in graphics, electronics, food technology and a range of examination choices. The buildings have undergone great change in the last decade, with two additional technology multimedia workshops being created to accommodate the higher number of pupils in the School. The department has purchased advanced CNC and laser cutting equipment to cement its place firmly in the 21st Century and to enable it to continually improve the quality of the products the boys produce.

The Chief Executive of the Design and Technology Association said "*The continuing popularity of the subject at GCSE is not surprising. Students choose it because they see the relevance to their lives and they enjoy the opportunity to develop their own ideas and apply maths and science in practical ways. It is also very pleasing to see the continued and significant increase in entry at AS level and the stable A level entry. The growing acceptance of the subject as a useful entry requirement for engineering degrees recognises the rigour and challenge of the subject in its own right and its ability to complement other subjects.*"

Design and Technology remains a popular subject choice in the School.

R. Baker

Food Technology

Food Technology – a fresh new department.

The new secondary curriculum, introduced from September 2009, placed an emphasis on cooking, diet, nutrition, health, and healthy eating. From September 2011 Food Technology was to become compulsory as part of key stage 3 Design and Technology. AGSB invested £3,000 in the construction of a new suite and it opened in July 2011 for a select few boys during Activities week. From September 2011 all boys have the opportunity to develop their culinary skills in the *Licence to Cook* programme. The picture shows boys already well practiced in cooking!

Roger Ashton-Griffiths was a character actor, screenwriter and film director. He began as a singer with the English National Opera then went into films and television.

Ian Hargreaves worked for David Cameron, has contributed to Radio 4's *The Moral Maze* and still writes articles on Murdoch and the press. A founding board member of Ofcom, he is now Professor at Cardiff.

Notable Old Boys:

Paul Allott
Paul Allott enjoyed a highly successful career as an opening bowler for Lancashire and England during the 1980s. He is featured in this book on page 75.

Alan Barnes
Alan Barnes is one of the country's leading jazz musicians. He attended AGSB in the 70s before going to Leeds College of Music in 1977 to study saxophone, woodwind and arranging. Wikipedia lists approximately 50 discs to his credit.

Over the years Alan has won many British Jazz awards in alto, baritone, clarinet and arranging categories. In 2001 and 2006 he received the prestigious BBC Jazz Instrumentalist of the Year award and in November 2003 was made a fellow of the Leeds College of Music.

Everyone was delighted when he returned to Altrincham recently for a gig at the nearby Cinnamon Club. Not only did the Swing Band have a master class with Alan in the afternoon, they then opened the evening's entertainment at the Cinnamon Club and Alan and one of his band members played with them too.

What an amazing experience for AGSB musicians!

Graham Brady
In 1997 Graham Brady was elected MP for his home constituency of Altrincham and Sale West, becoming the youngest Conservative MP. When the Conservative Party was in opposition he served in a variety of shadow ministerial posts - a spokesman on education, as the Parliamentary Private Secretary to leader Michael Howard and as Shadow Minister for Europe.

On 29th May 2007 he resigned his post in opposition to the policy on Grammar Schools of the new leader David Cameron. He said "*faced with a choice between a front bench position I have loved and doing what I believe to be right...there is in conscience only one option open for me.*"

Since then Graham has been a highly effective backbencher. In 2010 he was elected Chairman of the 1922 committee and in that role he represents the views of all Conservative MPs at regular meetings with the Prime Minister. In December 2010 Graham won the much coveted 'Backbencher of the Year' Award from the *Spectator* magazine.

Ian Brown & John Squire
Ian and John co-founded 'The Stone Roses' in the 1970s and their first album followed in the 1980s. They had a massive influence on music, bringing 'indie' music to their audiences. They changed the image of Manchester for a generation. In 1996, Ian said: "*Having spent the last ten years in the filthiest business in the universe, it is a pleasure to announce the end of the Stone Roses.*" However in 2011 'The Stone Roses' decided to reform and their pending tour in 2012 sold out just 14 minutes after going on sale.

Ian Livingstone & Steve Jackson
Ian and Steve used their love of fantasy games to create 'Tomb Raider' and 'Lara Croft', and a host of games such as 'Dungeons and Dragons'. Ian admitted that he is a 'games freak', but believed that helped in the success of the Eidos Company because he understood the language, the games which would not succeed and could recognise innovative development teams. He appreciated the cultural differences too *Japanese have big production values, the French like adventure games, English prefer fighting games and a bit of humour, the Americans like more polished games.*

Eric Mensforth was a leader in the engineering industry and a pioneer in the development of the helicopter. He built the Dragonfly which was chosen for the Navy's first Helicopter Squadron.

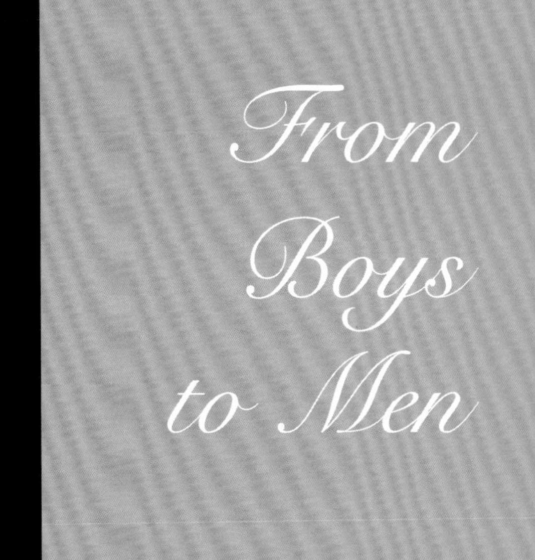

Other Old Boys:

Roger Ashton-Griffiths Film actor.
Sir Robert Booth Chairman of the National Exhibition Centre.
Prof Gerald Dix Lever Professor of civic design at Liverpool University 1975-88.
Hugh Freeman Psychiatrist and editor of the *British Journal of Psychiatry* 1983-93.
Ronald Gow Dramatist, actor, playwright.
Prof Ian Hargreaves Editor of The *Independent* and *The New Statesman.*
John Hopkins Conductor of the BBC Northern Orchestra 1952–57.
Edward Horley Chairman of Governors, Mayor of Altrincham.
Rev Prof Leslie Houlden Professor of Theology at King's College London 1987-94.
Rev Prof Barnabas Lindars Rylands Professor of Biblical Criticism at Manchester University 1978–90.
John Lowry CBE President of British Association of Oral and Maxillofacial Surgeons.
Sir Eric Mensforth CBE Chairman of Westland Aircraft.
Rev Prof John Morill Professor of British and Irish History at Cambridge University.
Tom Ross 2010 Labour Party Candidate for Altrincham and Sale West.
G.S. Smith Silversmith, jeweller, engraver; the success of the Norton motor bike in the Manx T.T. came from his invention of the first aluminium cycle chain not to stretch.
Fred Talbot Weather forecaster on ITV.
Prof Roger Warwick Professor of Anatomy at Guy's Hospital and former editor of 'Gray's Anatomy.'
Dylan Wiliam Professor of Education, London University. He believes passionately in raising standards through teachers, by helping students to become better learners.
Steven Williams broke a world record for Tiddlywinks in 1966 which was reported in the Guinness Book of Records.

Peter Ellis

In 1988 – during the last days of the Berlin Wall a small boy worries about a house move and a new start in school. The first thing that struck him on arrival here 22 years ago was the warmth of the community here. It seemed to exist in a bubble of old fashioned decency, fair play, and high expectations. It was comforting and reassuring. Coming back for interview two years ago, more than the infrastructure felt familiar.

"I was shown around with courtesy, I could hear the other teachers enjoying their jobs, but I couldn't hear the pupils much at all. Quite a few of my old teachers were still here and welcomed me.

The Head Master's office where the critical conversation took place had much the same feel, and the same furniture. Even the Science labs smelt nostalgic. The boys want to work and want to be helpful; the School is twice the size it was in 1988 and the students come from a much wider range of ethnic backgrounds. Everyone is trying a bit harder, and is a bit more under pressure, after only 20 years. But, I like it."

Peter Ellis is now teaching Classics at AGSB.

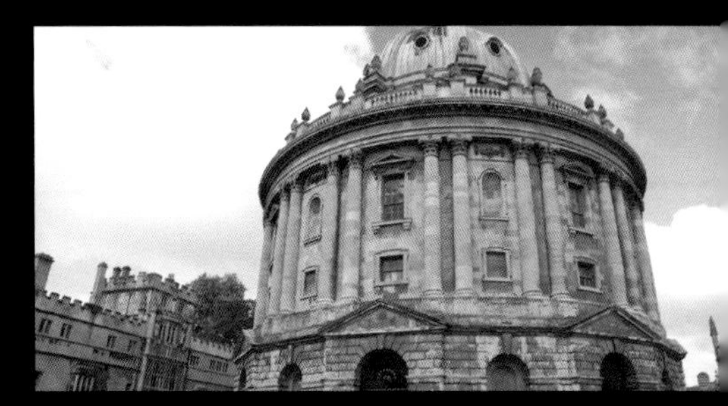

Letters from Old Boys:

From Germany: *"I was commissioned from Sandhurst into the Royal Corps of Signals and I now command an armoured troop of 27 men and eight vehicles. I enjoy the life enormously, especially adventure training. Being at AGSB broadened my horizons and helped me achieve what I have."*

From London: *"I am reading English at King's – one of the first institutions to place value on English Literature and the first to view American Literature with any seriousness."*

From Oxford: *"University is an enormously valuable and enjoyable experience. Sixth Form at AGSB is a half way house, a time to take on responsibilities which prepare you for life after school. Perhaps the most important skill you need is time management and the likely outcome of this being that you will work efficiently under pressure."*

From Nottingham: *"There are more representatives of AGSB here than at any other university. One student is secretary of the Entertainments Committee, one secretary of the History Society, one Editor of the Engineering Society magazine, one Captain of the Fencing Club, one Treasurer of the Union. We also have members of the University chess team, basketball team and tennis team."*

11+ question

Mary is 12 years old and her father is 42. How old will Mary be when her father is ten times as old as Mary was 6 years ago?

11+ question

A man covers 5/8 of a journey by train, and 1/6 by boat. His train journey is 44 miles longer than by boat. How long is his journey?

Despite its present secure and unassailable position as one of the best Grammar Schools in the Northwest, over the decades Altrincham Grammar School for Boys has experienced many years of uncertainty, thwarted plans, and very little money available for improvements. There have been several occasions when amalgamation with the Girls' School seemed inevitable, and even when the School was opened in 1912, it was suggested that the Boys' and Girls' Schools would share the same site. It was realised though that the Girls' School grounds at the Devisdale would not be big enough, and Lord Stamford donated the present site on Marlborough Road for the Boys' School to be built.

In 1912 the School had five teachers and 57 pupils, but within the first few years the number of boys increased four-fold, and the problems of accommodation required desperate measures. Despite the start of the First World War, extra space was needed; the bike shed, an Army Hut and the library became classrooms. After the War, new buildings were authorised and built, but by 1930, the success of the School meant that our accommodation was once more overcrowded.

During the next few years a Hall and a Gym were built (this is now the Music Room) but investment in schools was patchy and the building programme negligible. Boys were taught in totally inadequate conditions. During the Second World War, no money was available for school buildings and it wasn't until 1954 that the School acquired a new dining hall. The old dining hall was transformed into labs and the bike shed into a metalwork room.

Marlborough Road had to be constructed in 1912, but even by 1960 there was no pavement or tarmac and it had a great many potholes. Since there was little passing traffic and no parked cars, it was not an urgent problem, but money for improving the road was not forthcoming. However, it did have a splendid line of trees instead. A few more buildings were added during the 60s, such as the old gym (which was demolished in 2008), but the future of the School was becoming a pressing and crucial issue. In 1974 Trafford Metropolitan Borough was created, so AGSB was no longer a Cheshire school. Discussions about the future of the School turned once again to the possibility of amalgamation with the Girls School. Councillors believed that numbers would fall and predicted that by 1990 the School would only have 400 boys on the roll. The vigorous suggestion by Trafford that the Devisdale was the appropriate site for amalgamation was regarded by the cynics as having more to do with the price our 28 acres of valuable land would fetch than any educational principles.

A public meeting was arranged, but members of staff were not allowed to be involved (and so contradict the speeches delivered by the Director of Education). Fortunately the parents started a campaign to save the School – a vote showed overwhelming support for retaining the School. A meeting in London was arranged with the Education Ministers and, on the basis of the evidence submitted by the school representatives, it was decided the School would not close while it still had 'sufficient' numbers. The majority of parents preferred two single sex schools, but a considerable injection of money was needed to improve the deteriorating state of the buildings. The next plan which was to turn the School into a Comprehensive secondary school was overthrown by one vote, but amalgamation plans were still being considered. A second deputation from the School went to London to present a case for the status quo. The projected number of boys was made out to be 500, but this was far too low. More classrooms were required to accommodate the rising numbers, and the existing buildings improved. Things moved slowly, then in 1990 the Head Master received the all important letter stating that "*the two Altrincham Grammar Schools are to remain on separate sites*" The Head Master, Mr Nodding, described it as our "*Annus Mirabilis*" – AGSB would remain here at Marlborough Road as the only Boys' Grammar School in the Borough.

In 1990, after years of no new buildings, AGSB took on Local Management for Schools (LMS) to become responsible for deciding how the School's money was spent. The number of boys was rising rapidly, including a record number in the Sixth Form. Improvements over the previous decades had been minimal and, in 1994, Ofsted inspectors were shocked by the dilapidated buildings. In 1995 a ballot of parents voted for Opting Out, so the school became self- governing. Following the change of government in 1997, Grant Maintained Schools took on Foundation Status in 1999, but the freedom the bursar and the Head Master had enjoyed under Grant Maintained Status remained. Over the past 15 years they have been able to manage the income as efficiently as possible in order to balance the requirements of teaching the boys, improving the existing buildings and expanding facilities to cater for the ever growing number of boys and rising expectations.

In 2010 it was a natural progression to accept the Conservative Government's offer of Academy Status, which confirmed the School's independence – for the time being AGSB is an independent state funded school but who knows what the next change will be. What is certain is that whatever its status, AGSB will retain its strong educational ethos.

11+ question

A farmer started to plant 10 rows of cabbages at 10.15am. He planted the first 6 rows at a rate of 5 rows in 25 minutes, the last 4 rows at a rate of 3 rows in 33 minutes. When did he finish?

And finally . . .

The following student and staff photographs are supplied by courtesy of H Tempest

Form 7BY

Form 7SQ

Form 7JY

Form 7WD

Form 7KD

Form 8DR

Form 7NW

Form 8EW

Form 8HE

Form 9EL

Form 8HN

Form 9HA

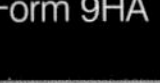

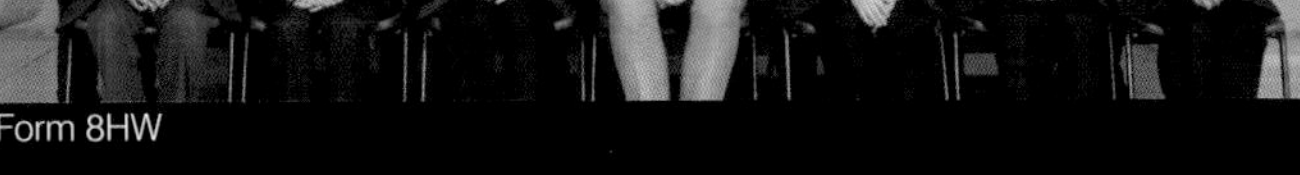

Form 8HW

Form 9HR

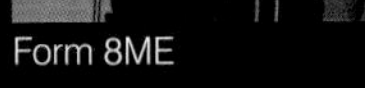

Form 8ME

Form 9KL

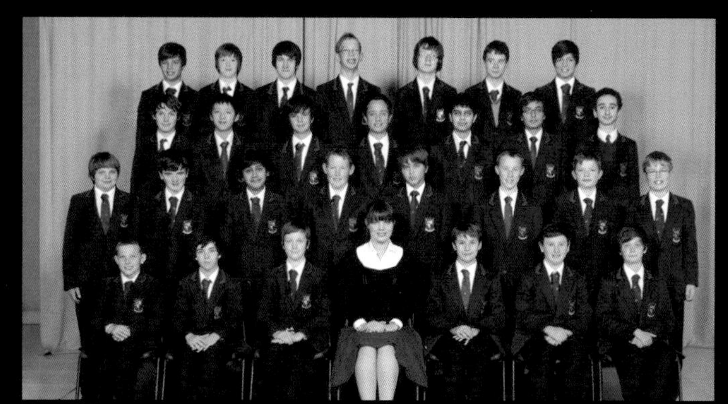
Form 9LY

Form 10BK

Form 9PS

Form 10MA

Form 9RF

Form 10PT

Form 9SY

Form 10RD

Form 10SN

Form 11MK

Form 10WY

Form 11MN

Form 11EY

Form 11PR

Form 11GT

Form 11RN

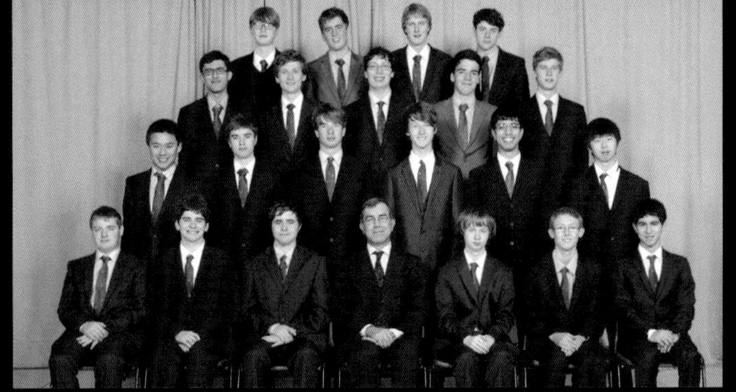

Form 12AZ

Form 12CN

Form 12HD

Form 12KS

Form 12MD

Form 12MR

Form 12ST

Form 12WX

Form 13BN

Form 13SM

Form 13CT

Form 13TL

Form 13GD

Form 13TM

Form 13MG

Form 13WG

Head Master

Tim Gartside

Governors:

Chairman: Christopher Barrat
Vice Chairman: Nick Evans

Duncan Battman
Khumi Burton
Marion Dodds
Sharon Forster
Tim Gartside
Denise Haddad
Terry Hall
Mark Herrington
Darren Jones
Karen Lord
Tim Lowe
Sharon Kupusarevic
Judith Nicol
David Ormesher
James Pearson
Andrew Shaw
Charles Streuli
Malcolm Thomson
Caroline Shield
Gary Harding

Clerk to Governors:
Jacqui Durrington

Nader Ahmadzadeh

Ali Alsaadi

Robert Baker

Laura Barratt

Brian Bennett

Pauline Bewley

Garry Binns

Darren Birtwell

Jane Bold

Sue Bracegirdle

Neil Bradley

Vicky Brennan

Kathryn Bushnell

Rashenda Chapman

Sarah Chase

Janet Clarke

Karen Crowther

Rob Cummins

Keith Dalby

Declan Danaher

Elena de Jesus

Elizabeth Eastwell

Glyn Eaton

Peter Ellis

Linda Eyers

Staff of 2012

Mary Farrell

Richard Gittins

Robert Gledhill

Andrew Hagon

Eddie Hall

Ellie Harper

Sibylle Harris

Therese Harvey-Voyce

Mandy Heathcote

Mark Herrington

Mark Heslop

Fraser Heywood

Belinda Hochland

Pauline Howell

Joanne Hutchinson

Stephen Jelly

Kamil Kaminski

Marian Keall

Chris Kidd

Nicola Kielty

Hilary Knowles

Sue Knowles

Andrea Lacon

Raquel Lago Costa

Dianne Landsborough

Astrid Lavin

Nichola Lawless

Sarah Lawrey

Karen Lord

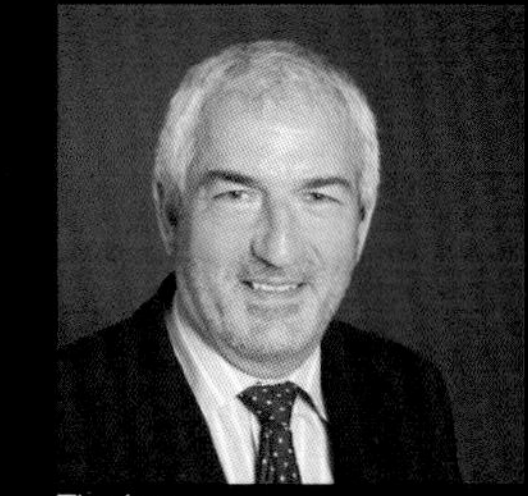
Tim Lowe

Charlotte Maguire

Julian Marsden

Lucy Mattison

Hilary Meadowcroft

Scott Meakin

Suzanne Meehan

Nicholas Mellor

Carly Moran

John Moran

Kevin Morris

Tom Murray

Ginny Murray

Colin Myers

Caroline Newton

John Newton

Brian O'Flynn

Connie Orford

Sally Passey

Ann Pearson

Kevin Pearson

Stuart Peet

Robert Perkins

Kate Potter

Helen Pracy

Chris Rawson

Absent from staff photos:

Staff of 2012

Claire Raffo
Yuhong Zhang
Pauline Capel
Peter Birrell
Phil Lee
Mark Taylor
Claire Mahony
Anna Leigh

Gavin Reeder

Tracey Richardson

Lesley Saunders

Caroline Shield

Helen Short

Tim Shorten

Darren Smith

Steven Squire

Kevin Stephen

Helen Stewart

Vicky Sully

John Taylor

Emyr Thomas

Holly Thompson

Jan Timmins

Joanna Tomson

Alison Underwood

John Wales

Clifford Webb

Andrea Welsby

Pauline Wilcox

Alan Williams

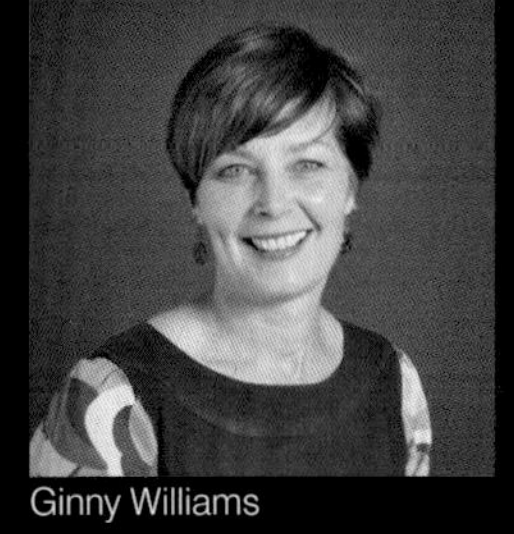
Ginny Williams

Gill Williamson

Michael Wingate

Joshua Branch, Daniel Lockett, Ismaile Chaudhary, Oliver Carroll

Head Boys & Deputies 2011-12

Head Boy	Daniel Lockett
Deputy	Joshua Branch
Deputy	Ismaile Chaudhary
Deputy	Oliver Carroll

Head Boys during the last 50 years

1963 – 64	A. Kerr
1964 – 65	J Smith
1965 – 66	W Morton
1966 – 67	K Knowles
1967 – 68	J Lyons
1968 – 69	M Haworth
1969 – 70	D Chester
1970 – 71	G Richards
1971 – 72	D Meacock
1972 – 73	J Ulbrecht
1973 – 74	S Warburton
1974 – 75	R Vos
1975 – 76	P Darbyshire
1976 – 77	A Fiske
1977 – 78	C Gray
1978 – 79	P Thomas
1979 – 80	S Miller
1980 – 81	P Davies
1981 – 82	S Pollard
1982 – 83	C Biddle
1983 – 84	R Roe
1984 – 85	R Seymour
1985 – 86	N Bowker
1986 – 87	C McKinlay
1987 – 88	D Adderley
1988 – 89	J Lightbody
1989 – 90	M Prest
1990 – 91	D Lightbody
1991 – 92	A Barnes
1992 – 93	S Mabon
1993 – 94	J Brown
1994 – 95	A Galbraith
1995 – 96	J Hope
1996 - 97	A Allen
1997 – 98	M Davis
1998 – 99	W Allen
1999 – 00	S Burnside
2000 – 01	A Delaney
2001 – 02	D Smith
2002 – 03	T Keevil
2003 – 04	D Mitchell
2004 – 05	D Stratton-Powell
2005 – 06	D MacFadden
2006 – 07	A Shakespeare
2007 – 08	B Gani
2008 – 09	O Marsh
2009 – 10	M Nicol
2010 – 11	C Graham
2011 – 12	D Lockett